THE WORLD ACCORDING TO
GORE

THE WORLD ACCORDING TO
GORE

DEBRA J. SAUNDERS

ENCOUNTER BOOKS
SAN FRANCISCO

First edition published in 2000 by Encounter Books, an activity of Encounter for Culture and Education, Inc., a nonprofit tax exempt corporation.

Encounter Books website address: www.encounterbooks.com

Manufactured in the United States and printed on acid-free paper.

The paper used in this publication meets the minimum requirements of ANSI/NISO Z39.48-1992 (R 1997) (Permanence of Paper).

Library of Congress Cataloging-in-Publication Data

Saunders, Debra J., 1954–
    The world according to Gore / Debra J. Saunders.-- 1st ed.
      p. cm.
    ISBN 1-893554-14-7 (alk. paper)
    1. Gore, Albert, 1948- 2. Gore, Albert, 1948---Political and social views. 3. Vice-Presidents--United States--Biography. 4. United States--Politics and government--1989- I. Title.

E840.8.G65 S28 2000
973.929'092--dc21
[B]   00-031622

10 9 8 7 6 5 4 3 2 1

To my parents,
Barbara Ellen Barrett Saunders
and Jeremiah James Saunders

Contents

Tobakka

Both in our personal lives and our political decisions, we have an ethical duty to pay attention, resist distraction, be honest with one another and accept responsibility for what we do—whether as individuals or together.

—Albert Gore Jr., *Earth in the Balance*

CHICAGO 1996: The Democratic National Convention was hopping. Clinton's advisers, trying to contrive some news to keep the media interested, had decided to buck the tradition of having the vice president appear only on Thursday, the last night of the convention, to introduce the president. Instead, Al Gore would deliver a speech on Wednesday night. This extra time in the spotlight was a generous gift from President Clinton in reward for loyal service during the first term.

Gore led with a self-deprecating joke about "the Al Gore version of the Macarena," in which he just stood there in straight-faced parody of his wooden stereotype instead of shaking his booty to the bawdy tune, as delegates had been doing. He could kid about being boring because this vice was connected with his chief virtue of being morally upright, or stiff, but in the right way, and because it showed that his main interest was in getting down to business. Gore declared that Bob Dole was "a good and decent man" who warranted respect, then dismissed the GOP nominee as "a bridge to the past." He warned against the ominous forces who "want to replace Bill Clinton" because of the president's progressive politics and railed against opponents who "want to outlaw all affirmative action and many other measures to reach out to those who want to reach up"—an allusion to Proposition 209, a California ballot measure that would ban government racial and gender preferences.

Then he talked about his sister.

Or more precisely, he talked about the death of his sister, the vivacious Nancy Gore Hunger, who had succumbed to lung cancer in 1984 at the age of forty-six. Gore blamed her death on "an invisible force" that was "considered harmless" when she started smoking at age thirteen, before the link between tobacco and cancer had been firmly established. He spoke of the family's later efforts to get her to stop, "but she couldn't." He spoke of being in the room when his sister died and the helplessness of being able to do nothing more than tell her that he loved her.

Gore's voice resonated with pain for his sister and concern for others as he said, "Tomorrow morning, another thirteen-year-old girl will start smoking. I love her too. Three thousand young people in America will start smoking tomorrow. One thousand of them will die a death not unlike my sister's. And that is why *until I draw my last breath*, I will pour my heart and soul into the cause of protecting our children from the dangers of smoking."

As the vice president finished, the convention hall erupted in applause. Some cheered Gore for what they saw as his courage in revealing this highly personal story. Others—I was one of them, in the press gallery covering the convention for the *San Francisco Chronicle*—were struck by the drama of the occasion, even if they felt that talking about so private a matter in so public and political a venue came close to exploiting one's family for partisan gain, and thus crossing a line which most politicians treated as inviolable.

When he was struggling to win re-election in 1992, for example, President Bush did not try for sympathy votes by bringing up the tragic death of his little daughter Robin, who succumbed to leukemia when she was three—not even after Gore callously trashed him and Vice President Dan Quayle for opposing the Family Leave Act. Not even when Gore asked, "Is it because they don't think it's a family value for the child's parent to be there amid the pain and suffering and confusion and fear? Or is it because their lip service to family values is totally outweighed by the thought that the wealthy, powerful and privileged might be unhappy if they had to give that employee time off?"

Yet Gore's anguish over his sister seemed genuine. I realized that we now lived, for better or worse, in a tell-all era in which personal revelation was not only permissible, but even expected from public figures. Gore may have been implying that personal pain should dictate public policy—a notion frowned upon by earlier generations, who believed that cool heads, not raging hearts, should set policy—but at least he seemed sincere, and I could certainly understand how a sister's death would lead him to want to use his office to prevent similar tragedies. And after all, he was part of a generation that believed the personal was political.

I ran into Joe Cerrell Jr. late that night at a convention shindig. Then a White House aide to Gore, Joe was beaming. It had been clear to me for some time that Gore had inspired great awe and loyalty in Joe—not something every politician can say of his relationships with his aides. It was clear that Joe thought his boss had hit a home run in his speech. He asked me what I, a known Republican, thought of it.

3

My answer was something like this: I disagree with Gore's decision to say what he did, but you can't help but be struck by the guy's decency.

Then the next day, I read something that changed my mind altogether about Al Gore. While he had led America to believe that he had an epiphany about the homicidal nature of cigarettes after his sister's death in 1984, it turned out that in 1988 he had nonetheless campaigned for president extolling the virtues of tobacco farming. Stumping in North Carolina, he told tobacco farmers, "Throughout most of my life, I raised tobacco. I want you to know that with my own hands, all of my life, I put it in the plant beds and transferred it. I've hoed it. I've chopped it. I've shredded it, spiked it, put it in the barn and stripped it and sold it." According to an account I read later, Gore even drawled out "tobacco" so it became *tobakka*—the way growers pronounced it—to show that he was one of them.

When Gore had excoriated the tobacco industry the previous night, he also failed to mention that for several years after his sister's death, he received and cashed annual checks from the family's tobacco farm. (According to Gannett News Service, the Gore family continued to grow tobacco or lease the family's tobacco allotment to another farmer until 1991.) Also, Gore took political contributions from tobacco political action committees as late as six years after his sister's death. He entered the vice presidency supporting a federal program that yields higher prices for tobacco growers. Nor could Gore use ignorance as an excuse for this support. As he had just revealed to the entire country, he knew from painful personal experience that tobacco kills.

In 1984, *the year his sister died,* Gore helped the tobacco industry fight a move for strong anti-tobacco labeling by pushing for a compromise that dropped the words "death" and "addiction" from the proposed warning label. While still in the Senate, he had voted against a measure proposed by his then-colleague

Senator Bill Bradley to raise the federal tobacco excise tax because he didn't want to hurt the tobacco farmer. In 1985 Gore voted to sell 1.2 billion pounds of surplus tobacco to Big Tobacco at a cut rate. In 1988, he voted against restrictions on tobacco advertising.

In *Inventing Al Gore,* Bill Turque chronicles the Gores' creation of a family mythology about its relationship to tobacco. Al insisted in conversations with reporters that he sold his tobacco allotment in 1989. His father, demonstrating the Gore willingness to use family to score political points, told reporters he realized he should stop growing tobacco in 1991 when his grandson Albert III, then four years old, asked him, "Isn't that what killed Aunt Nancy?" The only problem was, as Turque writes, "Albert III turned four in October 1986, five years before the allotment was actually sold."

In other words, Gore used his sister's death in his operatic denunciation of smoking with full knowledge that he had grown tobacco, courted tobacco growers and remained throughout his political career a staunch defender of government subsidies for the cash crop. Worse yet, he was so cynical about the stunning contradiction between his words and his actions that he felt free to mount a soapbox and denounce *other people* for putting their financial interests before the welfare of children.

I was struck as much by the arrogance of Gore's convention speech as by its hypocrisy. Surely he must have known the press would uncover the facts and question how the former tobakka man could claim that personal tragedy had transformed him into the Noble Anti-Tobacco Warrior. Surely he must have known the press would uncover his long and fruitful ties to Big Tobacco that continued for years after Nancy Gore Hunger's death. Or just maybe Gore—and perhaps even his handlers, who were paid to know better—thought that his political persona was so upright and ethical that no reporter would dare challenge his ties to tobacco, even as he was carping at Republicans for being addicted to tobacco money.

At a luncheon the day after his convention speech, reporters demanded that Gore explain himself. His answer was even more stunning than his assumption that he should skate unscathed through all his past associations with tobacco: "I felt the numbness that prevented me from integrating into all aspects of my life the implications of what that tragedy really meant."

A numbness—a numbness that lasted some six years—prevented him from doing the right thing. A numbness so deep and long-lasting that Gore was taking tobacco money even as he was writing *Earth in the Balance*, a book in which he excoriated other politicians for putting what served their political interests ahead of what they knew was right, a book which he dedicated to his sister.

▲

For many Americans, Al Gore crossed a Rubicon in his 1996 convention speech. They watched him that Wednesday night on television and believed that he was exactly what his public image suggested: a more wooden but also far more sincere and moral version of Bill Clinton. They were moved by the brave sense of loss he displayed in speaking of his sister and by the political resolve born of emotional pain. But by the next day, as news about his ties to Big Tobacco tumbled out in a series of press reports and Gore descended into psychobabble in an effort to explain his post-epiphany behavior, everything changed. Al Gore lost his halo.

Like others, I could never look at him as the earnest Boy Scout again. He had become more complicated, but less admirable. He had revealed fault lines in his political personality that demanded exploration.

In front of all America, Gore had delivered not exactly a fib, not exactly a flip-flop, not exactly a tactical lie, but something worse: an outright fabrication that brazenly exploited the death of his only sister. He had ransacked the sacrosanct realm of private experience only to debase its authenticity.

Memories of this speech weighed on me even more as I began to work on this book. One nagging question came up again and again: Given his tobakka past, what had made Gore believe that he could get away with representing himself on television as an ardent tobacco foe since his sister died in 1984?

I began to see other examples of a giant gulf between what Gore did and what he said. Of course, other politicians are guilty of this sin. But when caught, most of them sheepishly rationalize any disparity between position and action or attribute it to political "evolution." Gore was different. He simply denied that his own past existed.

I began to think of this syndrome as the Gore Disconnect. I thought of the many political professionals who worked for Gore and knew about his strong ties to Big Tobacco but didn't try to stop him from portraying himself as a born-again tobacco foe. Even if the vice president believed that he could get away with this pose, surely someone in his operation had to know that journalists would dredge up his past remarks and expose the venal side of the grieving brother. Was Gore so much a victim of his Disconnect that he would not listen to warnings? Or were his advisers as blinded as so many of Gore's supporters were by the conviction with which he spun out his narrative?

It was not until December 1999 that I felt I had finally gained insight into this question. *Meet the Press* host Tim Russert was moderating a debate between Gore and Democratic primary challenger Bill Bradley. Feeling vulnerable in the early primaries, Gore immediately went on the attack. On various points he misrepresented Bradley's position or his record. He charged that Bradley's health plan would provide health care "vouchers" for adults that were "capped" at $150 per month, when the plan actually provided tax credits, not vouchers, and had no hard and fast cap. He excoriated Bradley for doing little about campaign finance reform in his first seventeen years in the Senate, although Bradley in fact had been a co-sponsor of campaign finance reform legislation since 1985. He accused Bradley of opposing "our participation in Bosnia," even though Bradley had voted in favor of troop deployment three times.

Gore also charged Bradley with sins of which he himself was equally guilty, if not more so. He attacked Bradley for making a campaign promise that consumed the non–Social Security surplus, when his own promises did the same. He criticized Bradley for negative campaigning, when his own campaign had already attacked not only Bradley's policies, but also Bradley personally for being a quitter in deciding to retire from the U.S. Senate.

None of those facts mattered, however, and Gore seemed to be downright indignant as he hammered away at Bradley, who feebly tried to defend himself.

I asked myself again as I had in 1996: Why did Gore act so self-righteously, with such contempt for the very behaviors in which he himself had engaged? The answer was that this technique had worked for him throughout his career.

For all its distrust of the media, the public believed that surely if Gore were guilty of the same shortcomings for which he had scolded Bradley, the press would report it the next day in banner headlines. But news organizations have severely underreported Gore's many and substantial contradictions. Most reporters have tended to take him at his word—assuming that if he were lying, and certainly if the lies were as large as opponents claimed, someone else would have written about it. Thus when Bradley first charged at a New Hampshire debate that Gore had been a pro-life legislator, a reporter later told me, the pressroom groaned. As he explained it, those covering the debate either believed Gore's haughty denials or figured that if the charge were true, it was not relevant because Gore was clearly very pro-choice now.

Sometimes it seems that Gore's unblinking audaciousness— as seen in his pose as a fiery campaign reformer despite his 1996 fundraising abuses—has left journalists breathless, unsure how to describe the apparent gap between what he says and what he has done. A March 12, 2000, *New York Times* headline announced, "Gore to Embrace Campaign Finance as Central Theme," with the subhead, "Acts on a Vulnerability." The story, by Richard Berke and Katharine Q. Seelye, leads with the assessment that this was an "audacious attempt to turn one of his greatest vulnerabilities into an asset." At times one senses that reporters and editors may secretly want to yell "Phony!" Then again, I have wondered if Gore is so convincing in his certainty that reporters have begun to doubt *themselves* for doubting him.

Then there's the fact that Team Gore knows how to handfeed the news to journalists. After the December *Meet the Press* debate, many uncritical press accounts focused on Gore's dramatic challenge to Bradley to forego paid advertising through the remainder of the primary season. Few focused on Gore's misleading statements about Bradley's record, or his own. One paper even ran a story about how the 1999 primary was turning out to have less mudslinging than was seen in previous elections. Others uncritically reported Gore's promise not to run personal attack ads or to assail Bradley personally—as if he had not already trashed Bradley.

Sometimes it seems that the majority in the press believe it is wrong to write about Gore except from a limited number of journalistically approved themes. There's the boring wonk angle, the stiff orator angle, and that one-time favorite, the good politician who is so oppressed by having to serve under an alpha male president that he has been reduced to hiring a number of gurus to tell him what to wear.

There have been amusing, and deserved, opinion pieces about Gore's mind-boggling fabrications—kissing cousins of his convention speech about his sister—such as his assertion that he helped to invent the Internet; his exaggerated claim that Tipper and he were inspirations for the main characters in the novel *Love Story*; his claim that he helped bring light to the Love Canal story, although the hearings he credited for highlighting the eco-scandal occurred some two months after area residents had been relocated; his assertion that he was a "principal proponent" of the Earned Income Tax Credit, when he was a late co-sponsor of the measure; and his claim to have been a co-sponsor of the McCain/Feingold campaign reform bill, even though it was introduced after he had left Congress. Gore's habit of giving himself too much credit led pollster John Zogby to observe, "The boastfulness could be worrisome for him. It's almost as if there is a self-esteem problem there."

There have been articles about Gore's decision, despite his positioning himself as a foe of Big Tobacco, to hire people from the cigarette industry such as his top media consultant, Carter Eskew, finance director Tina Flournoy, a former Philip Morris executive, and his fund-raiser Jonathan Tisch of Loews Corporation, which owns Lorillard Tobacco. Reporters discovered that the affluent Gores, who frequently speak of the need to help others, gave only $353 to charity in the year 1997 when he earned $197,729. Still, only when the primary heated up, and Bill Bradley finally decided to make Gore's truthfulness an issue, did reporters begin to focus on the vice president's almost programmatic lack of candor about Bradley's record and his own.

There also has been too little coverage of Gore's thought. Other than Jerry Brown, and arguably Newt Gingrich, there probably is no other contemporary politician who can match

Gore for pumping out ideas, position papers and proposals about government and the social world in which we live. Gore has written a book about the environment. Almost a decade ago, he advocated "completely eliminating the internal combustion engine over, say, a 25-year period." He has developed a highly detailed plan to make the suburbs of America more "livable." He has a plan to provide access to health care to every child in America by the end of his first term. He has pushed for more federal involvement in local government and in family life, saying the government should help middle-class families juggle their busy schedules. Gore is a strong proponent of federal industrial policy and a long-time supporter of a long list of corporate welfare programs. He advocates universal preschool. He wants Uncle Sam to require employers to give workers time off to visit their children's schools. He has championed a national three-digit number (211) that would allow cell-phone users to dial for traffic information wherever they are in the country. He frames all of these proposals in a near-apocalyptic urgency, leading his daughter Karenna to explain that "he basically wants to save the world." She might just as easily have said that he basically believes the world *needs* him to save it.

This book offers a roadmap to Goredom. It examines the Gore Disconnect and evaluates Al Gore's political history and his ideas in an attempt to get beyond what he says and decipher what he thinks, what he really believes, what kind of government he wants for America, and what kind of president he might actually be.

CHAPTER ONE

Triple Smart

A college friend once lamented that Albert Arnold Gore had been "deprived of childhood" because, as the son of a famous man, he did not enjoy carefree years as a boy. Yet almost from his birth in Washington, D.C., in 1948, Gore was not just a son, but also a junior member of a loving partnership. "When I was growing up, it never once occurred to me that the foundation upon which my security depended would ever shake," he once explained. His parents provided a bedrock of security and stability, not to speak of expectation, that allowed Gore to feel a sense of his own importance throughout his life.

If much was required of young Gore, much was given to him, too. His was a unique—and uniquely political—upbringing. As a boy, he once eavesdropped on a phone call from President Kennedy to his father, Senator Albert Gore of Tennessee, after which he professed to be shocked by JFK's salty language. Aware of the virtues of bipartisanship, he also once sat on Vice President Richard Nixon's lap as Nixon presided over the Senate.

His sister Nancy was ten years old when the thirty-six-year-old Pauline Gore found herself expecting this second child. She regarded the pregnancy as something of a miracle, especially when it yielded the male heir she and her husband had been hoping for. Young Albert would allow the family name to continue and provide a fallback position for his father's political aspirations. Before Albert's birth, his father had badgered the local paper, the *Nashville Tennessean*, into running a page one story if Pauline Gore had a boy. As biographer Bill Turque noted in his book *Inventing Al Gore*, the paper complied with a story headlined: "Well, Mr. Gore, Here HE Is—On Page 1." At the father's insistence, the son was named Albert Arnold Gore, with the stipulation that he could become Junior later on if he so chose.

In 1956, Al Gore Sr.'s name was put in nomination for vice president at the Democratic National Convention. The senator never made it onto the Democratic ticket, but he always saw in the second Al Gore a second chance to make it to the White House. Gore's mother, Pauline La Fon Gore, brought her own considerable gifts to this project. She met her future husband when she worked as a waitress to pay her way through Vanderbilt Law School, the second woman ever to attend. She was unable to find employment as an attorney in Tennessee after she graduated, so she practiced oil-and-gas law in Texarkana before she returned to Tennessee to marry, have a daughter and wait for a boy.

"We raised him for it," his father boasted when Gore joined the Clinton ticket. "He has been groomed from childhood to be president," one of Al Jr.'s big donors once boasted. Said a long-time supporter, "He's been running for president since he was in the tenth grade."

Make that since the first grade, according to a profile in the *Washington Post*. At the age of six, Young Albert convinced his father to buy him a 98-cent bow and arrow instead of a 49-cent bow and arrow, as they originally agreed. The Gores were so proud of their son's negotiating skills that they called the *Knoxville News-Sentinel* and got a story in the paper: "There may be another Gore on the way toward the political pinnacle. He's just 6 years old now. But with his experiences to date, who knows what may happen." After Albert had talked his father into buying him the more expensive toy, he told his mother, "Why, Mama, I out-talked a senator." The paper accompanied the story with a photo of young Gore, his dad, and his bow and arrow, along with the assertion that "Al Gore is a young man to be watched from here on in."

Starting in the fourth grade, Albert attended Washington's prestigious St. Albans Episcopal School for Boys. There, as one classmate later put it, he was "more loved by the headmaster than his peers." While his father served in Congress, Gore spent most of the year living with his parents in an eighth-floor apartment on Embassy Row's elegant Fairfax Hotel. He was "finished" by extensive foreign travel. To help their boy learn Spanish, his parents sent him to Mexico one summer. They also shipped him to France and Switzerland to improve his C average French.

Gore spent his summers making an entry for a future campaign biography at the family farm in Carthage, Tennessee. His father, who gave him a pony named Flame, believed that future presidents ought to be able to boast of youthful farm chores when they ran for office, and he worked his son hard. So in fact, Gore really did do farm chores, as he later claimed when running for president. If he exaggerated, it was within an acceptable human margin, as when he told the *Des Moines Register* that his father had taught him "how to clean hog waste with a shovel and a hose. He taught me how to clear land with a double-bladed ax. He taught me how to plow a steep hillside with a team of mules. He taught me how to take up hay all day long in the hot sun and then, after a dinner break, go over and help the neighbors take up hay before the rain came and spoiled it on the ground." Still, there was time left over for Gore to learn such barnyard arcana as how to hypnotize chickens.

In 1999, Gore recited his farm chores in the Iowa primary to trump Democratic rival Bill Bradley in the contest over who had had the most authentic non-political "life experiences." But if his memories of hard work, sweat and muscle aches were real, his portrayal of himself as a barefoot farm boy was not. Gore grew up well aware that he was not being raised for an adulthood of shoveling hog waste, plowing hills and taking up hay. Everyone in the family, in his schools and in his home town knew he was destined for politics.

In Washington, where he spent most of his youth having nothing whatever to do with hog waste (at least that produced by real pigs), Al Gore was known as a serious young man, dutiful, courteous to adults, a grownup at an early age. He was considered a grind at St. Albans, just as he later became a detail-oriented wonk on Capitol Hill. Remembering young Albert's "earnest admonitions" to fellow students in the refectory, the *Washington Post*'s David Ignatius, who attended St. Albans behind Gore, wrote, "No man has changed less in 35 years than Al Gore." Michael Kinsley was saying the same thing when he famously dubbed Gore "an old person's idea of a young person."

Al Sr., a graduate of the school of hard knocks, worked to raise a son with a more erudite speaking style and worldly demeanor, a better version of himself, wearing the right school tie and possessing a fluency in languages and the arts. In effect, he ceded victory to his son in the Oedipal struggle, enabling Young Al to see himself as the more polished Gore, the more intelligent Gore, and indeed the better Gore. For instance, father and son had a running argument as to the cause of the common cold, with the younger Gore telling his father that only germs, and not cold weather, were responsible for colds, leaving the senator with the thankless job of trying to refute him. In high school, Young Al tried unsuccessfully to scold his father into throwing political caution to the wind and casting a vote for the 1964 Civil Rights

Act. Underneath an apparent reverence for his father, the son was able to enjoy a strong sense of both moral and social superiority.

Ranking twenty-fifth in his class of fifty-one boys, Gore was nevertheless so sure of himself that he applied to only one college, Harvard. Many writers enquiring into this period of his life have concentrated on Gore's long hair, pot smoking and disenchantment with politics after his first year as freshman class president; but *San Francisco Chronicle* managing editor Jerry Roberts remembers him as a formidable student. Roberts was a year behind Gore at Harvard, where they both lived in Dunster House. "He was an excellent pool player," Roberts recalls. "He was good at everything he did."

They had a term for guys like Gore. "There was this phrase that we used in Dunster House, I don't know how widespread it was, but you called people Triple Smart," Roberts explains. "Because everyone was smart at Harvard. You had to be smart to get there." Gore was Triple Smart because he was good academically and he had a sense of the real world. Roberts particularly remembers an analysis Gore wrote about the National Security Council apparatus at the Kennedy White House. "I remember being struck by the fact that he had a depth of understanding and knowledge about that kind of thing, that world, and power was second nature to him," said Roberts, who admits that at that point in his own life he thought "foreign affairs was going out with a French girl."

Gore took a freshman seminar led by Martin Peretz, the future owner of the *New Republic*, who was to become his political mentor and chief cheerleader. In his senior year, he attended a seminar conducted by Harvard Institute of Politics director Richard Neustadt that appeared to reawaken his temporarily dormant interest in politics. Gore also attended a science class taught by geophysicist and oceanographer Roger Revelle, one of the first scientists to theorize that industry had increased the concentration of carbon dioxide in the atmosphere and that this might lead to global warming. Another of Al's professors, famed psychologist Erik Erickson, had a thesis on "generativity"—"the ability to care for many others and to establish and guide the next generation"—that also had a long-term influence on him. Gore didn't shy away from using his family connections as a student any more than he would later on as a politician; so when he wrote his senior thesis on the impact of television on the presidency, he was able to interview Bill Moyers, James Reston and Arthur Schlesinger Jr.

While Gore never discouraged people from believing that he was a high-achieving student with grades to match his triple-smart demeanor, the *Washington Post* reviewed his Harvard transcripts as part of its 2000 campaign coverage and found that the contrary was true. "In his sophomore year at Harvard, Gore's grades were lower than any semester recorded on [Texas Governor George W.] Bush's transcript from Yale," the paper reported. For two years, Gore placed in the lower fifth of his class. While he later would style himself as an expert on scientific and technological issues, Gore received a D in Natural Sciences as a sophomore, and a C+ in that subject as a senior.

After his freshman year at Harvard, Gore stayed away from student-body politics—the epitome of uncool in the 1960s—but also avoided the anti-war activism that kept the campus in turmoil. Instead, he kept his eye on Washington and on his father's career. When the Senate Foreign Relations Committee held hearings on the military buildup in Vietnam, Al skipped classes for two or three days to watch approvingly as Senator Gore railed against the war.

In 1968 he attended the Democratic National Convention in Chicago, where he helped his father write his convention speech. But this achievement was not enough. It was also at this convention that Gore first showed his penchant for taking credit for things with which he had little or nothing to do, a tendency that would grow over time. For years afterward, as he was trying to build his own political legend, he told people that *Chicago Sun Times* columnist Charles Bartlett had interviewed him, then passed his statements about "the end of an era," the need for a "prompt end to the war" and for "young Americans" to be involved in politics on to Vice President Hubert Humphrey's speechwriters, who inserted many of Gore's thoughts verbatim into Humphrey's speech to delegates. When *Washington Post* reporters David Maraniss and Ellen Nakashima checked into the story, then told Gore that Bartlett denied passing on Gore's statements to Humphrey or even having any link with Humphrey in 1968, he blithely shrugged off his claim as the result of a "faulty memory."

As a senior at St. Albans, Gore had begun going out with a vivacious young blonde he first met when she was on a date with a fellow student. She played the drums for an all-girl band called "The Wildcats" and drove a blue Mustang. Her name was Mary Elizabeth Aitcheson, but everyone called her Tipper. A stunning looker who wasn't stuck up about her good looks, Tipper was a high school senior when Gore first brought her to the family farm to meet his parents. When it was time for her to apply to college, Tipper naturally looked toward Cambridge, applying to nearby Garland Junior College, which she attended for two years before transferring to Boston University, where she majored in psychology. Throughout her college years, Tipper's real major was Al Gore. She spent so much time in Cambridge, she might as well have enrolled at Harvard herself. Tipper and Al became engaged on the banks of the Charles River. But marriage was not the only big move that Gore had to consider upon graduation. After spending years proudly telling friends about his father's opposition to the war, he also had to decide what to do about Vietnam.

The Martyr

They were two figures on horseback. The son had enlisted in the Army and was about to be sent to Vietnam, a war he thought was morally wrong. The father, a U.S. senator, rode upright, astride a white stallion. He too objected to the war; still, he turned to his only son and advised him, "Son, always love your country."

The moment was staged for a campaign ad that aired on Tennessee televisions during Al Gore Sr.'s 1970 re-election campaign. First elected to the Senate in 1952, Gore Sr. was in big trouble. Unlike most of his Tennessee constituents, he had opposed the Vietnam War early on. While his son had failed to coax him into voting for the pivotal Civil Rights Act of 1964, the senator had supported other civil rights laws, including the 1965 Civil Rights Act, which many white Tennesseans also opposed. Yet it was his remoteness, as much as his politics, that got Gore into electoral hot water. Many voters had come to see their senator as more a creature of the Northeastern establishment than of Possum Hollow. Especially after Teddy Kennedy threw a post-Chappaquiddick fundraiser for Gore, wags had taken to calling him the third senator from Massachusetts. A former teacher in a one-room schoolhouse who had worked his way through college, then studied law at a night school at the Nashville YMCA, Gore had used his law degree to cover a lot of territory since his days growing up on a hardscrabble Tennessee farm. Now he stood to lose the position, power and prestige that he had gained through hard work, determination and political smarts. He did not want to let go. His triple-smart son did not want him to let go either.

While the great majority of his fellow graduates of Harvard's Class of 1969 found ways to evade military service in Vietnam, Young Al found himself in a unique situation. While his parents reportedly had told him they did not want the senator's close electoral contest to influence his decision, the dutiful son could not help but think that if he evaded the service, he might doom his father's chances of holding onto the Senate seat that was so important to them all. So he enlisted in the Army after graduation, becoming one of only two graduates from his Harvard class to enter the service. He was thinking politically even then. While Gore later would say that he volunteered so that he would not have to live with the thought of a different son of Carthage serving in his place, it was clear to those around Gore that he went to Vietnam to help his father's re-election. This gesture would bolster his father's image as a loyal American, whose patriotism had never swerved, regardless of his opposition to the war. It was one of the few times in his life when Young Al went against the grain. He was one of only 28 among 234 draft-age sons of members of Congress to serve in Vietnam.

During his months stateside before finally shipping out, he spent many weekend furloughs campaigning for his father in uniform. But their joint effort to hold the Gore Senate seat fell short. With help from the Nixon White House, three-term Republican Representative Bill Brock defeated Al Sr. in a hard-fought contest that featured what many observers saw as thinly disguised race-baiting designed to attract the George Wallace vote. The son blamed his father's loss on "subliminal smut" from the Nixon crowd. Defiant in defeat, the senator proclaimed, "The causes for which we fought are not dead. The truth shall rise again." It later would become clear that the "truth" to which he was referring was his own son.

The day after the election, the two men took a canoe ride on the Caney Fork River. The heartbroken senator asked his son, "What would you do if you had had thiry-two years of service to the people, given to the highest ability, always doing what you thought was right, and had then been unceremoniously turned out of office? What would you do?"

Al answered, "I'd take the thirty-two years, Dad."

It was mature advice, yet his father's defeat seared Young Al and indelibly defined his approach to constituent politics. While other men with life experiences similar to his own might have said later on that they were shaped by serving in Vietnam, or by the death of a beloved sister, the significant event for Al Gore was the voters' rejection of his father in 1970. The experience triggered what he later described as his first "long dark night of the soul." It is as if his father's election loss so outraged Young Al that, Scarlet O'Hara-like, he vowed that he would never experience electoral rejection again. Following that blow, he would define justice as victory, and political defeat as the greatest injustice of all.

Throughout his adulthood, Al Gore has described how his father's defeat and his own service in Vietnam had soured him as a young man on politics. Later, when he became a politician himself, he praised his father effusively, and often grossly exaggerated Gore Sr.'s "courage" in putting his beliefs before his career.

When Gore Sr. died in 1998 at the age of ninety-one, he had lived to see his son stand one step away from the great goal, the one they had jointly pursued for so many years. The vice president stayed up all night to write a eulogy in which he called his father "the greatest man I ever knew in my life." He explained, "My father was brave. I mean really brave. He opposed the poll tax in the forties, and supported civil rights in the fifties. By the time he was in his final Senate term, I was old enough to understand clearly the implications of the choices he made when he repeatedly rejected the advice of many fearful political allies who had urged him to trim his sails. He was proud to support the

Voting Rights Act of 1965. He was damned if he was going to support Haynsworth or Carswell, Nixon's suspect nominees for the Supreme Court. And I was so proud of that courage."

The last advice his father gave him, Gore said, was, "Always do right."

Gore's constant emphasis on his father's willingness to sail against the wind might lead an observer to assume that the admiring son had determined to follow his father's example, no matter what the personal cost. But to examine Gore's career is to conclude that Gore drew exactly the opposite conclusion from the lacerating 1970 defeat. In his book *Gore: A Political Life,* Bob Zelnick surmises that the lesson Al learned from his father's electoral loss had to do less with principle than with pragmatism—with what happens when a Southern politician appears to have swerved too far to the left, leaving his constituents feeling that he has abandoned them.

Thus Young Al, regardless of the positions he may have held personally, always took pains to position himself as a centrist. As a young Representative, he called himself "a raging moderate." He was compulsive in his visits to Tennessee and his attendance at town meetings there, taking pains to be the good son for the people of his state as he had been for his parents. As vice president, he continued to nurture his political grass roots, returning home to make important political announcements in Carthage. He would align himself with the occasional progressive cause, such as environmentalism, but he tried to avoid treading on his constituents' bedrock beliefs.

In putting his father on a pedestal, Al had gotten the old man in a safe place. In fact, after his political days were over, the former senator had not sought out opportunities to behave nobly and selflessly. Even while in the Senate, the elder Gore had a penchant for allowing fat cats anxious to ingratiate themselves with a powerful senator to pay top dollar for the Angus cattle he raised. As Bob Zelnick writes, "Residents will tell the inquiring visitor of how lobbyists and others with an interest in Gore's work would parade to Carthage during the fall auction period, bid outrageously high prices for Gore's stock, and sometimes not even bother to pick up what they had purchased." International industrialist and sometime Soviet tool Armand Hammer—memorably described by the Center for Public Integrity as a man who "personified the worst excesses of both capitalism and Communism"—put Gore Sr. on the payroll of his New Jersey cattle business when Gore was still a member of the House in the 1950s. When FBI director J. Edgar Hoover wanted to prosecute Hammer for his pro-Soviet activities, Gore took to the Senate floor to defend Hammer against allegations of bribery that later were proven to be true.

After Tennessee voters retired the senator, Hammer named Gore Sr. president of Island Creek Coal Company and vice president of Occidental Petroleum, jobs carrying six-figure salaries that eventually reached an estimated $500,000 annually, a true windfall in the 1970s. The former senator revealed the size of the chip he still had on his shoulder when he explained to a friend, "Since the voters of Tennessee have chosen to send me out to pasture, I intend to graze in the tall grass." Hammer also bought and then sold to Gore Sr. the farm that he turned around and quickly sold to Al and Tipper. Hammer had paid $160,000 for the farm; they paid $140,000 for it—after it had been discovered that the property contained zinc deposits and Gore Sr. had worked out a deal for Occidental to pay $20,000 per year for rights to the zinc. As the Center for Public Integrity reported in *The Buying of the President 2000*, "Perhaps even more astounding than Hammer's decision to sell the land and pay royalties is that Occidental never actually mined the land. In 1985, Gore began leasing the land to Union Zinc, Inc., a competitor of Occidental's. Gore still receives $20,000 a year in royalties. In all, the

Hammer-engineered sweetheart deal has put hundreds of thousands of dollars in profits in Gore's pocket."

Nor did the largesse stop there. According to a memo by White House aide Harold Ickes, Occidental gave $50,000 to Al Gore after one of the vice president's White House dialing-for-dollars ventures. The *New York Times* reported that Occidental gave $100,000 more after its chief executive was allowed to spend two nights in the Lincoln bedroom.

In his book *Earth in the Balance,* Gore later railed against America's bad "habit" of using natural resources at "an ever-increasing level of consumption." He was particularly dismissive of what he called "enablers"—to wit, "those who will not acknowledge these destructive patterns." Yet since 1974, he has earned some $450,000 from his annual zinc contracts.

▲

In a borrowed Army dress uniform, Al Gore married Tipper at the National Cathedral in Washington, D.C., in 1970, the Gore family's *annus horribilis*. The newly hitched couple walked down the aisle to the tune of the Beatles' "It's All Too Much."

For several months, Al and Tipper lived in a trailer in Alabama, near Fort Rucker, where Gore was stationed. The experience of living in a trailer park and watching base helicopters blow their laundry off the clothesline would later serve as proof that they had not always lived lives of privilege. About to ship off to Vietnam to save the family name, young Al pressed his friends to read the science-fiction classic *Dune*, about the prescient son of a powerful Duke, who goes to war to save a faraway planet from destruction.

Gore spent five months in Vietnam as a reporter assigned to a non-combat engineering brigade. His accounts of his service at times have been, like so many aspects of his life, embroidered. He told journalist Gail Sheehy, "I took my turn regularly on the perimeter in these little firebases out in the boonies. Something would move, we'd fire first and ask questions later." He told a friend about seeing women and children cut in half by Huey helicopters. But *Los Angeles Times* reporter Richard A. Serrano talked to a number of vets who served with Gore, and concluded that Gore "often portrayed his experience as more dangerous than it truly was." Even this is an understatement. In fact, Gore was never close to combat and never saw an American casualty.

Conservative critics have charged that Gore used family influence to get light duty and that he was watched over by other soldiers. Gore may have glossed over the things he did that helped him get assigned as a journalist—for example, he enlisted in Newark, where there was no shortage of administrative jobs—but with his degree in government from Harvard and his high military test scores, he didn't need to pull strings to be assigned to non-infantry duty.

It is also true that by the time Gore got to Vietnam, the military had begun pulling soldiers out. After three months, he sought and won a waiver to return to the U.S. to attend Vanderbilt Divinity School.

While in Vietnam, Gore sent Tipper stories he wrote for the Army newspaper. She passed one of them, "Fire Base Blue is Overrun," to *Tennessean* editor John Siegenthaler, who ran it in his paper. Siegenthaler had a history of hiring the children of the great and powerful, including the sons of Arthur Schlesinger Jr., the daughter of Hank Aaron, and David Kennedy, doomed son of RFK. He also hired Gore as a reporter while he was attending divinity school part time. After failing to complete five of the eight courses he took—eventually earning Fs in those classes—Gore gave up studying theology.

While Gore worked as a journalist, his father was working

on adding "businessman" to his son's political resume. The senior Gore and a friend created Tanglewood Home Builders to sell residential properties on land young Gore had bought for $45,224 in 1969. As a young reporter Gore also bought his farm, rich in Armand Hammer's zinc and conveniently located in his father's old congressional district.

In looking back on his career as a reporter and later an editorial writer, Gore has exaggerated his journalistic accomplishments, just as he did his military experiences, boasting to the *Des Moines Register* that he "got a bunch of people indicted and sent to jail." Actually, Gore's big investigative piece concerned a black city councilman named Morris B. Haddox who took a $300 payoff in an undercover sting. (Biographer Bill Turque discovered that the story led one black leader to accuse Gore and his paper of "attacking the whole political structure of our black community.") The first jury deadlocked; a second jury failed to convict Haddox because jurors believed he had been entrapped by prosecutors collaborating with Gore's *Tennessean*. It was said that the verdicts crushed Gore, who shortly afterward took a leave of absence and started law school. Yet twenty-five years later, Haddox would be a supporter of Gore's presidential campaign and Gore would tell a reporter that Haddox was "an innocent man, because he was not proven guilty."

Like his farm chores and Vietnam experiences, Gore's stint as a journalist became a crucial entry in his curriculum vitae. The journalistic legend he created went like this: When he first started working in the newspaper business, he was soured on public life because of Watergate, Vietnam and his father's defeat. Taking a job with his hometown paper, he was looking for reconnection. At first he refused to cover politics at all. After he relented and agreed to cover City Hall, he saw the good that government could do. And it was this happy realization that led a reluctant young man who otherwise shared some of the disillusionment of his generation to enter public service.

The Smartest Boy in His Class

Just as he never finished divinity school, Gore failed to get his law degree. This is because the job he really wanted became vacant in 1976 when Representative Joe Evans, the congressman for a district including much of the area his father once represented, announced his retirement. Gore determined to run for the seat on the day the news broke. Despite the legend Gore has constructed, his friends and *Tennessean* associates were not surprised. Perhaps the only person who was surprised by the turnabout was Gore's wife, who preferred private life to public campaigning.

The daughter of parents who divorced when she was three, in an age when divorce was rare, Tipper was raised by her single mother and her maternal grandparents. Her mother suffered from mental illness and was hospitalized twice. These challenges left Tipper hungry for a stable family life. She told the *New Yorker*'s Elsa Walsh that when they married, "we both wanted six children." When they wed, she had planned on becoming a counselor for children. In the early years in Tennessee, she enrolled in a master's program in psychology. Then she began taking a photography class, and found what she thought was her calling. She had a part-time job as a photographer at the *Tennessean*. "I was as happy as I had ever been," she told Walsh. Then her husband decided to run for Congress. She told him she would campaign for him on her days off. He told her that with nine candidates in the field, that wouldn't do. A reluctant Tipper found a cousin to care for Karenna and hit the campaign trail. Later, when they lived in Washington, she would build a darkroom in the house and take up freelance photography, only to drop it again, as the demands of motherhood and her husband's political career overtook her life.

She would always be ambivalent about politics, yet always game to do whatever was necessary to advance the Al cause. In the spring of 1999, when polls showed that Al's numbers among women were inexplicably low, Tipper went on NBC's *Today* show to give a wife's-eye view of her husband. "He doesn't stay in anything very long when we go to bed," she giggled. The couple also smooched and hugged in an interview with *Washington Post* gossip columnist Lloyd Grove, who wrote that "they playfully suck face every time the camera is pointed elsewhere."

In that first run for Congress, Young Al did not ask for help from his father, who was still saddled with his reputation as an Eastern establishment liberal, but he was happy to have his mother stumping for him. His father was hurt, but he also did his part, pulling strings behind the scenes. Young Al won handily campaigning as a moderate Democrat with the help of the Gore name recognition and Gore connections. He claimed that he didn't want people to vote for him because of his father, but as family friend Walter King Robinson told him, "That's probably the only reason they will."

In late 1999, when he was sagging in some polls against Bill Bradley and George Bush, Gore gave political reporters a parable of how hard that first congressional race had been. He told the *Houston Chronicle* that he was the underdog in 1976, expected to finish "back in the pack"; but just as it was wrong to count him out then, so he shouldn't be counted out in the 2000 primary. Similarly, he told the *Boston Globe*, "I was expected to finish seventh in a nine-person race. And Tipper and I beat them with shoe leather." Shoe leather? Try money and a famous family name. At the age of twenty-eight his net worth, thanks to his father's association with Armand Hammer, was already more than $250,000 (in 1976 dollars); thus he was able to lend or give his own campaign more than $100,000.

As a Southern congressman, Gore held frequent town meetings and carefully staked out moderate positions calculated to endear him to his district and make his seat safe. He pushed to have House proceedings televised. He opposed military aid to the Contras in Nicaragua, but supported humanitarian aid. He cast pro-life votes and he opposed gun control legislation. He conducted hearings on organ transplants. In 1981, he opposed the Reagan tax cut. He had a role in developing the 1980 Superfund bill that dealt with cleaning up chemical spills and toxic dumps. But it was his mastery of the intricacies of nuclear disarmament and his advocacy for eliminating multiple warheads that cemented Gore's growing reputation as a triple-smart intellectual/politician.

It was when a group of girls told him that they expected a nuclear war in their lifetimes that he decided to learn all there was to know about arms control. By all accounts, he was an absolute grind, spending several hours each week studying or being briefed on the issue. His hard work paid off. Gore became a key player in 1983 and 1984 in a compromise with the Reagan administration that saved the MX missile.

Reporter Judy Fahys, now with the *Salt Lake Tribune*, remembers meeting Gore when she was a graduate student in journalism, interested in learning more about missiles. Most politicians weren't interested in talking to someone at her level, who probably couldn't do much more than get a small piece into an out-of-town paper. But Gore enjoyed talking about warheads. Running into the congressman in a Capitol Hill hallway, Fahys asked him about the difference between single-warhead—of which he was a proponent—and multiple-warhead missiles. He said he would be happy to explain the missile situation if she wanted to accompany him to a meeting. They drove through town while he talked enthusiastically about the issue, pleased to be able to demonstrate his expertise.

"He was smart. It wasn't about politics. It was really about ideas," says Fahys, who remains impressed with Gore's excitement over the minutiae of missiles. "He wasn't trying to advance his career by telling me this. He had nothing to gain."

Yet many of his colleagues had a different view of Gore at that stage of his career. "He was arrogant," one Democratic congressional aide described him. "He loved being the best-looking and the smartest boy in his class and he felt he didn't need [his colleagues] to succeed."

▲

When GOP Senator Howard Baker announced his retirement in 1984, Gore ran for Baker's seat and handily won it. In the Senate, Gore continued to work on his reputation as one of the best and brightest members of Congress. He made headlines by digging up proof that NASA had cut back on its quality monitoring of booster-rocket O-rings after the Challenger blew up in 1986. He went to Brazil to check out the destruction of rain forests. He supported the Reagan incursion into Grenada, thus styling himself as a centrist on national security. Democratic operative Ann Lewis gave him this backhanded compliment to the *Washington Post*, "What is most characteristic of Gore is that he takes a highly technical issue, masters it and promotes it with a view toward maximizing its potential for media attention."

Moving into the role of up-and-coming wife who would be a socially-involved asset for an up-and-coming politician, Tipper also courted attention from the media after hearing some highly sexually-charged lyrics in her daughter's music collection. In 1985, she got together with other Washington wives to found a group called the Parents' Music Resource Center, which launched a crusade for voluntary warning labels on sexually suggestive music. The crusade so rattled the music industry that it volunteered to put "Explicit Lyrics—Parental Advisory" labels on certain albums. At first, Tipper's group rejected the offer, not wanting the industry to control the labeling process. But after music moguls painted the group as overly censorious, the PMRC agreed to the deal.

Tipper also wrote a book, *Raising PG Kids in an X-Rated Society*. She felt that she had found a cause that could cross ideological lines by appealing to moderates and conservatives concerned about the over-sexualization of the rock scene, and to liberals concerned about the misogyny of rock lyrics. What's more, the issue allowed her to reinforce her strong feminist leanings without offending the men or women who distrusted the National Organization for Women.

In September 1985, the Senate Commerce Committee held hearings on the issue, which allowed Tipper and Al to work as a tag team. The *Los Angeles Times*'s Sara Fritz later wrote, "To those who attended, the hearings will long be remembered as one of the most brazen efforts on the part of any committee to generate news coverage." While Al was attacking entertainment types for being "really irresponsible in promoting suicide and all the other things we have heard about here," Tipper testified that her group did not want to censor Hollywood or pass laws muzzling Hollywood, but simply wanted voluntary labels. In his appearance, rock musician Frank Zappa called the Parents' Music Resource Center "a cult" and questioned the appropriateness of Tipper testifying before a committee on which her husband served. Gore left his wife twisting in the wind as he fawned over Zappa, telling him, "I have been a fan of your music, believe it or not. I respect you as a true original and a tremendously talented musician."

(How much of a fan was Gore? Years later, the *Times* of London would report that Gore similarly gushed over Courtney Love of the grunge band Hole at a Hollywood party. When he told her he was "a really big fan," the skeptical Love countered, "Yeah right, name a song, Al." The really big fan couldn't.)

▲

In 1988, at the age of thirty-nine, not yet having completed his first term in the Senate, Al Gore announced that he would run for the presidency. Tipper may have been the only person who was truly surprised. When her husband told her of his decision, she was on a book tour, which she promptly cancelled to join him. Years later, Elsa Walsh asked Gore if he had ever considered not running for the White House in consideration of his wife, who never really wanted to be in politics. He gave a strangely convoluted response: "She doesn't want me to make a choice that runs against what I feel called to do, and so if she were not convinced that I genuinely felt a calling to serve in this way she would definitely not want me to be in politics. But since she knows that I am who I am, then she wants to support me and make the best of it."

Gore felt he could run because he had won the support of Nate Landow, rainmaker for Democratic hopefuls. As Bill Turque later wrote, Landow "raised millions for Jimmy Carter in 1976 and was considered a shoo-in for an ambassadorial post until the story of his business relationship with Joe Nesline, a Washington gambler with ties to Meyer Lansky's organization, landed in the papers. Landow was never charged with any wrongdoing, but politicians who found their way to his door knew they weren't dealing with a champion of good government."

Gore campaigned for an increase in the minimum wage. He vowed that in a Gore administration, "Any government official who steals from the American people or who lies to the United States Congress will be fired immediately." He framed himself as a centrist Democrat, a committed environmentalist, and the "only active farmer in the race." In his announcement speech he called for putting men on Mars by 2000. Gore's father had a numerological theory about why his son would win. "In 1960, we went from the oldest president...to the youngest...and by sheer coincidence, in 1988, we have a chance to do that again."

With their eye on the White House, the Gores trekked to Hollywood for a crow-eating meeting, arranged by Democratic power broker Mickey Kantor, with thirty or so entertainment big-gies, including rock star Don Henley, TV producer Norman Lear and music producer Danny Goldberg. Tipper later said that she went to the meeting in order to explain that, no matter what some people thought, she never supported censorship. But the Gores actually went a little further than that, and unfortunately for them, someone at the meeting smuggled in a tape recorder that captured their remarks.

Tipper abjectly admitted to the group that the hearings her anti–rock porn campaign had inspired were "a mistake." Then, as *Variety*'s Henry Schipper reported, her husband "attempted to exculpate himself from the proceedings by virtue of the fact that he was a 'freshman minority member of the committee' in no position to veto the affair. Indeed, the Gores laid blame for the hearing at the door of two other senators—John Danforth (R-Mo.) and Paula Hawkins (R-Fla.)—both of whom Sen. Gore said were eager to hold the heavily publicized forum." Unfortunately for Gore, Schipper later checked the 1985 Congressional Record and found that not only had Gore openly praised committee chairman Danforth for convening the hearing, but he "was among the first to arrive and the last to leave, he questioned, often vigorously and at length, every witness or group of wit-nesses to come before the panel."

Tipper later told reporters that the episode backfired on the Gores because Hollywood types who "wanted to hurt me" leaked the story of the meeting. She insisted that the Gores didn't go to the meeting simply to make nice to contribution-rich Hollywood. But after the meeting Tipper did penance by working with industry nabobs to battle initiatives in twenty-two states calling for mandatory labeling of rock lyrics, thus fighting measures similar to what she had advocated three years earlier. This no doubt helped to turn the tide and open the wallets of Hollywood contributors in 1988 and subsequent years. The Center for Public Integrity later rated the Walt Disney Company, for instance, as Gore's ninth largest career patron.

If Gore was gentle with Hollywood, however, he was rough with his Democratic primary opponents. It was during a New York debate featuring Democratic primary candidates that Gore, while not citing the convicted killer by name, first brought up the issue of Willie Horton—a black murderer who raped a woman during a mistaken furlough from his Massachusetts prison—in an effort to discredit the eventual 1988 nominee, Massachusetts Governor Michael Dukakis. It was Gore who, in a Texas debate, attacked Dukakis for being soft on defense and overselling the "Massachusetts miracle"—another theme George Bush would pick up on the way to his landslide victory in November. At that debate Gore said, "The next president of the United States has to be someone the American people can believe will stay with his convictions. You gotta be willing to stand your ground and be consistent." To which rival candidate Representative Richard Gephardt countered that Gore should look at his own record: Gore had opposed an oil-import fee, then dropped that opposition when campaigning in oil-rich Texas. Said Gephardt, "Lately you've been sounding more like Al Haig than Al Gore." To which Gore shot back, "That line sounds more like Richard Nixon than Richard Gephardt."

It was in the 1988 race that Gore first revealed himself to be a ruthless competitor, having mastered the "subliminal smut" he so abhorred when Bill Brock turned it on his father in 1970. Gore's campaign ran a nasty ad hitting Gephardt for flip-flopping on abortion, an early example of the Gore Disconnect given the fact that Gore was guilty of the same change of position. The ad asked, "Who is the real Dick Gephardt?" Gore media also hit Gephardt with the charge, "As a candidate, he'll say or do anything to get elected." Another ad asserted that Dukakis "seems to say he wouldn't object to the Soviets establishing client states in our hemisphere."

Before the first primary vote was cast in 1988, Gore's press secretary wrote him a memo in which he warned that his image "may continue to suffer if you continue to go out on a limb with remarks that may be impossible to back up." Concerned about Gore's inflated claims about having been a real estate developer—Gore did own property that was developed, but real estate was hardly his career—his communications director, Arlie Schardt, wrote, "Your main pitfall is exaggeration."

Gore won five states—North Carolina, Tennessee, Kentucky, Arkansas and Oklahoma—in the 1988 Super Tuesday. Then came his Waterloo in New York. After endorsing Gore, Mayor Ed Koch started sniping at Jesse Jackson, and Gore piled on by complaining to a Jewish audience about Jackson's "embrace of Arafat and Castro." Together Gore and Koch managed to alienate both black and Jewish voters, and Gore's campaign began to flounder. He won 10 percent of the vote in New York, far behind Jackson, who had 37 percent.

It was an expensive, bruising experience for the first-term senator; in fact, it was the first election Gore had ever lost. Michael Dukakis later boasted, "I am the only person who beat Al Gore in an election." Gore's campaign was over.

Looking back at the experience, Gore concluded that his only misstep involved money—he had raised only $10 million—and decided he would never run for national office again without a fat bankroll. In this brief bid he had discovered the Rosetta stone of presidential politics: money, and the willingness to do whatever it takes to get it and use it to maximum advantage. He had also discovered that he possessed the stomach for hardball presidential politics, a quality so many of his contemporaries lacked. "You make the decision to run first," he later explained, "then...you're going to rip the lungs out of anybody who's in the race, and you're going to do it right."

Midlife Crisis

In April 1989, a year after his lacerating defeat for the nomination, Al Gore watched as his six-year-old son, Albert III, got hit when he ran in front of a car as the family was leaving a baseball game at Baltimore's Memorial Stadium. The boy was thrown thirty feet and badly injured. Gore and his wife Tipper spent the next month at the boy's side as he recuperated in the hospital.

"That experience has changed me forever," Gore told the Democratic National Convention in his 1992 acceptance speech, where he first experimented with merchandising the personal material he would use so cynically four years later. "When you've seen your reflection in the empty stare of a boy waiting for a second breath of life, you realize you weren't put here on earth to look out for our needs alone. We're part of something much larger than ourselves." It was his son's narrow escape from death, Gore later wrote in *Earth in the Balance*, that "made me increasingly impatient with the status quo, with conventional wisdom, with the lazy assumption that we can always muddle through."

In his early forties, Gore was having what he himself acknowledged as a midlife crisis. He had just lost his first election. No doubt the experience brought memories of his father's demise in 1970 flooding back. His son had almost died and was facing a difficult recovery. He and Tipper decided to undergo counseling.

His own therapy included writing *Earth in the Balance*, an effort to work through his angst over politics, life and himself. "I began to doubt my own political judgment," he wrote about the old Al Gore, "so I began to ask pollsters and professional politicians what they thought I ought to talk about." The new Gore who began to take shape in the pages of his book not only promised to be a committed environmentalist, but also said he would never pick issues by polls again. Just as his father had been too good for Tennessee voters in 1970, Gore emerged in *Earth in the Balance* as better than the politicians who beat him in 1988.

He decided not to run for the White House in 1992 because, he said, he wanted to spend more time with his family.

Gore's new interest in environmentalism merged with his old interest in psychology. As a student at Harvard, he had called America's anti-communism a "psychological ailment—in this case a national madness." In *Earth in the Balance* he linked abuse of nature and overuse of natural resources to "psychic pain." As vice president, continuing this psychologized approach to life and politics, he gave friends and reporters copies of *The Drama of the Gifted Child* by Swiss psychoanalyst Alice Miller—a book that dwells on the hardships of being an overachieving child—and routinely asked job applicants if they had read it.

Most politicians tend to be wary of introspection, seeing it as a cul-de-sac where ambition gets lost. Gore, however, made the rather public soul searching he used to resolve his midlife crisis a part of his political repertory. When he began his campaign for president in 2000, critics ridiculed his too-obvious attempt to play the role of "sensitive male." But they missed the extent to which his obsession with psychology seems tied to his belief that he has a special mission—messianic almost—to lead. He told a friend in San Francisco that God sometimes talked to him and that he had a "special relationship with Jesus Christ." As a vice president campaigning for the presidency, he admitted that he frequently asked himself, "What would Jesus do?" In his eulogy to his father, he spoke of the former senator as if to establish his own Christlike lineage: "He went into the world with peace. He held fast to that which was good. He rendered to no one evil for evil. He was of good courage. He strengthened the faint hearted. He supported the weak. He helped the afflicted. He loved and served all people who came his way."

Tipper, who'd gotten a master's degree in psychology, had a shorter take on Gore's drama. Asked about her husband's relationship with his father in a 1987 interview, she quipped, "You remember Oedipus?"

Gore had tried to please his father by running for the presidency, and he had failed. Gore had tried to be a good father himself, but his son had landed in the hospital. As he was recovering from his loss and refashioning a persona from the wreckage of these tragedies, he wrote a book about a world in chaos, a world in need of rescue, a world in need of a savior. It was a role that Al Gore Sr.'s son, tempered in a crucible of political defeat and personal tragedy, eagerly embraced.

▲

Gore's resolve to spend more time with his family in 1992 evaporated when Arkansas Governor Bill Clinton asked him to be his running mate. Gore was not the obvious pick for the vice presidency. The 1988 Democratic nominee, Massachusetts Governor Michael Dukakis, had chosen Texas Senator Lloyd Bentsen because he brought geographical as well as generational balance to the ticket. In 1992, Gore, a fellow Southerner and younger than the already young Democratic nominee, seemed unlikely to attract new votes for Clinton.

The balance that Gore brought had to with character and the reputation he had cultivated as a thinking man's politician. Where Clinton was smooth, Gore was earnest. Clinton excelled in empathy, Gore embodied the intellect. Clinton was slick, Gore was reserved. Where Clinton was instinctive, Gore was profound. Bill Turque writes that Clinton picked Gore in part because "Gore reminded him, in both intellect and temperament, of his most important political partner, his wife."

Gore also suited Clinton in that he too had fashioned himself in the New Democrat mode, as evidenced in his vote in favor of U.S. involvement in the Gulf War. Such a stand might be mandatory, Gore believed, for any Democrat who wanted to run for the White House in the future. Still, he knew that a debacle in Kuwait could haunt him forever. It was a difficult decision, but he crossed the Democratic leaders who opposed President Bush on the war, causing a furious Senate Majority Leader George Mitchell to stop speaking to him for months afterward.

Gore saw that joining Clinton would enable him to further define his moral profile. It was not so much a matter of behavior as of candor and accountability. When Clinton was asked in 1992 whether he had smoked marijuana, for example, he claimed, in an early warning of the slippery rhetoric to come, that he never inhaled. In 1988, on the other hand, Gore had admitted that he had smoked pot on an "infrequent and rare" basis, causing pundits to praise him for his honesty. It was not until 2000, when *Newsweek* began running excerpts of Bill Turque's *Inventing Al Gore,* that the media learned from John Warnecke, his fellow pot smoker, that Gore's marijuana use had actually been heavy and habitual, and had continued up until he ran for office. The way Gore handled the drug issue, therefore, turned out to be as characteristic of his modus operandi as Clinton's legalism had been of his.

As Clinton and Gore toured the country in 1992 with their attractive blond wives and school-age children, they crackled with the promise of the baby boom generation coming into power for the first time. They would do things differently and they would do things better. They would also say whatever it took to win the election.

Later on, Gore would acquire a reputation as a formidable debater. But when he faced the presumed lightweight Vice President Dan Quayle in 1992, he had his hands full and emerged from the confrontation only by lying about his record. By deftly dredging up facts from the past, which Gore baldly denied, Quayle brought the Gore Disconnect into full public view. During one exchange, for instance, Gore excoriated the Bush administration for using tax dollars to subsidize the moving of U.S. factories to other countries: "When are you going to stop using our tax dollars to shut down American factories and move 'em to foreign countries and throw Americans out of work?"

Quayle replied, "You know full well the Caribbean Basic Initiative, you've supported that."

"No," Gore replied, adding later, "I voted against it."

To which Quayle responded, "You voted for it and your record..."

"No," Gore insisted.

It simply wasn't true. Senator Gore voted for the program on April 24, 1990.

At another point, Quayle asserted, "At one time, and most of the time in the House of Representatives, you had a pro-life position."

Gore replied, "That's simply not true." But it *was* true. Once again, Quayle had elicited the Gore Disconnect, although it was not to become clear until eight years later how right he was on this point.

40

Pro-Life and Pro-Choice

In 1977, during his first term in the House of Representatives, Congressman Gore, who had learned from his father's defeat that he needed to appear in tune with Tennessee voters, supported a bill that would have denied federal funding for abortions even in cases of rape or incest unless the abortion was necessary to protect the life of the mother. In 1980 he voted in favor of a measure to prohibit health insurance packages for federal employees to cover abortions. In 1984, as he was running for the Senate, he voted in favor of the Siljander Amendment, which defined "unborn children from the moment of conception" as legal "persons" with civil rights protections. According to the National Right to Life Committee, Gore made twenty-seven anti-abortion votes while in the House and five pro-abortion votes, with one abstention. The Committee credited Representative Gore for voting pro-life 84 percent of the time, while the National Abortion and Reproduction Rights Action League (NARAL) rated him as voting against abortion 80 percent of the time.

When Gore made it into the Senate and began thinking about a run for the White House, his votes began to change. In 1988, running to the right of Michael Dukakis for the Democratic nomination, Gore said he supported abortion rights, but opposed "federal funding of abortion except in limited cases such as when the life of the mother is endangered." Gore got away with slamming Gephardt for flip-flopping on abortion, when he himself had done exactly that. An aide told *U.S. News & World Report*, "In effect, what we have to do is deny, deny, deny." And: "We've muddled the point, and with luck, attention will turn elsewhere"—which it did, because Gore was soon to drop out of the race.

Gore learned that Democratic primaries don't favor candidates who are not avidly pro-choice. By 1990 he had a 100 percent pro-abortion voting record. As Bill Clinton's running mate, Gore had rewritten his own abortion record in the same spirit that Stalin had Trotsky's image airbrushed out of a photo in which they both had stood near Lenin. "Senator Gore has always supported a woman's right to choose," spokesman Greg Simon told the *Washington Times* in 1992.

Through 1992 and 1996, Gore pretty much got away with his insistence that switching from an 84 percent pro-life voting record to a 100 percent pro-choice voting record did not entail changing his position on abortion. When he began his run for the presidency in 1999, he stuck to his story. In May of that year, the *National Journal* asked deputy campaign chairman Marla Romash, "Have any aspects of his stance on abortion changed over the course of his career?" She answered, "No, he has always supported a woman's right to choose." In an October interview with Sam Donaldson and Cokie Roberts on ABC's *This Week*, Gore falsely claimed that his support for the Siljander Amendment was "a procedural vote." He added, "And I've always supported *Roe v. Wade*"—even though giving the fetus civil rights would have seriously undermined that Supreme Court decision.

In January 2000, when Bradley hit Gore for changing his position, Gore responded that he had "always supported a woman's right to choose." Even when the press finally began reporting on Gore's abortion record he still stonewalled, refusing to admit to a change.

I witnessed Gore's detailed explanation of his votes in an editorial board meeting at the *San Francisco Chronicle* in February 2000. Gore was masterful. He explained that he had always supported *Roe* and felt it was fair to characterize his position as solidly pro-choice because when he first was in the House, many members said they supported abortion rights but opposed federally funding the procedures. Gore said,

I felt back in those days that the most intellectually consistent posi-
tion was to say, this is a personal choice, and the government should
have no role whatsoever, either in criminalizing the procedure or in
subsidizing the procedure, is the way I thought at the time. I changed
that view when I came face to face with the practical inequity that
resulted for many of my constituents who could not exercise the legal
right to choose if they did not have the resources with which to make
the choice. And so quite some time ago, I came out in favor of pub-
lic funding. That's still the minority position in the country, but I
feel it's the correct position.

For those who didn't know better, it was not only a smooth performance but a perfectly plausible explanation. It explained why
Gore could claim that he hadn't changed his position, even
though newspapers reported that he had. Better yet, it allowed
Gore to seem supremely thoughtful on an incredibly difficult
issue.

The only problem is that if Gore had supported *Roe* before
he was elected to the Senate in 1984, he never bothered to inform
the public. When Douglas Johnson of the National Right to Life
Committee heard this new version, he responded, "Can he point
to any statement on the public record when he expressed support
for legal abortion in general or *Roe v. Wade*? I haven't seen that.
It's not like the question didn't come up." When asked about this,
the best that Gore aide Chris Lehane could do was point to his
boss's refusal to support any proposed constitutional amendments intended to gut *Roe v. Wade*. Thus in pages of documenta-
tion, even Team Gore could not produce one pro-*Roe* statement
that Gore had made before he won his Senate seat.

Pro-lifers, on the other hand, had copies of Gore letters to
constituents that spoke of Gore's opposition to abortion as well as
federal funding of it. There was a quote in the *Nashville Banner* in
1976: "I don't believe a woman's freedom to live her own life, in

all cases, outweighs the fetus's right to life." There was the Sil-jander Amendment vote.

Mary Sharon, president of Tennessee Right to Life in the early 1980s, recalls meeting with Gore twice. She said that Gore told her he had been pro-abortion until the case of a notorious abortion doctor opened his eyes. He also told her that he was forced to reconsider his position when a national magazine showed a near-term fetus on its cover and his infant daughter kept pointing to it saying, "baby, baby." At first he tried to explain to her that the photograph was of a fetus. Then, he told Sharon, he finally said, "No, you're right, this is a baby." She adds: "And he explained to us that if his daughter knew it was a baby, then he knew it was a baby. He would just throw these stories in while we were discussing various laws."

The conclusion among pro-lifers who have kept an eye on Gore is that he used to be pro-life, but switched to the pro-choice side to enhance his chances of winning in a national race. As Matthew Rees of the conservative *Weekly Standard* wrote in a piece on Gore's abortion history, "Ambition trumped principle."

I think it's more a case of ambition trumping everything. And I believe the pro-lifers have it all wrong. Gore never really believed in the anti-abortion cause during the eight years he voted pro-life. He always knew that he would flip to the pro-choice side and so he cleverly constructed a paper trail over those eight years of pro-life votes, much as Bill Clinton did on the draft, to which he later could refer to explain his change of position.

In the House, the former divinity student had created argu-ments that were almost theological in their subtlety in order to accommodate not only an expected future conversion, but also his anticipated desire to claim that he had never really changed his position on abortion per se, but only on the narrow issue of federal funding. His constituent letters on abortion clearly were designed to give pro-life recipients the impression that Gore shared their views, yet they were written in such a way that Gore would be able to point to them in the future as proof that he had expressed doubts about the pro-life position. Their tone was rather legalistic and lacked the fervor of the true believer—the fervor present in his pro-choice rhetoric today.

In one stock letter, Gore wrote that abortion was "arguably the taking of a human life." A true opponent of abortion would not use *arguably*. Indeed, in 2000 Gore seized upon his use of this word as proof of his argument that he was not solidly pro-life in the House. Shown the letter, he told reporters, "I didn't write that. I didn't." He added, "I used the word 'arguably.' "

You have to credit Gore for thinking ahead. All those years ago, for four terms while he was in the House, he let his pro-life constituents believe he shared their views. He made sure that he never signed a letter that said he opposed legalized abortion itself. If you read his letters carefully—and ignored his vote in favor of the Siljander Amendment, as so many reporters have done—you could believe it was reasonable to characterize Gore's opposition as always having been limited to opposing federal funding.

Gore insisted to Dan Quayle in 1992—and has continued to insist—that he was never pro-life because he cannot conceive of himself as just another politician whose history on abortion "evolved" according to expediency. Yet his representation of his positions on abortion show that Bill Clinton, with his self-serving definition of sexual relations, was not the only master of deceptive language in this administration. It turns out that Al Gore was twenty years ahead of his mentor.

The Junior President

President Clinton gave Gore more power than any past president had ever given to his second in command. As Dick Morris put it, Clinton made Gore his "junior president." Specifically, Clinton ceded the environment, Russia, telecommunications, high tech and space to Gore. Just as Clinton had left the family finances to his wife, he left the governance of businesses to his vice president.

Gore's assigned areas of responsibility fit with his view of himself as a modern Renaissance man. He once spent a Fourth of July downloading pictures from Mars. As a senator he had introduced the Critical Trends Assessment Act, which would have created a $5-million-per-year Office of Critical Trends Analysis in the White House. Its purpose would have been to report "critical trends and alternative futures for the next 20 years" and to study economic, technological, political, environmental and demographic trends and their consequences. (An appalled Rushworth M. Kidder wrote in the *Christian Science Monitor*, "Even American corporations, which spend hundreds of millions analyzing the future, don't exhibit that arrogance.") Like Newt Gingrich, Gore has been a well-known fan of futurist Alvin Toffler, and Toffler has reciprocated, once gushing that Gore's most important contribution to the administration "is helping to wake America up to the fact that the world is changing."

Gore spent much of his second term trying to woo high-tech mavens and impress them with his own acumen. Smitten venture capitalist John Doerr told the *Los Angeles Times*, "When you walk into a meeting with him, his first question is, 'Just what exactly is going to be the future Java?' And he knows it's not a cup of coffee." On the 2000 campaign trail, Gore would show off to reporters the ease with which he operated his Palm Pilot. (This feat only left them confused as to why a man who maintained a legion of schedulers and handlers would need to keep a Palm Pilot.) His daughter Karenna called Gore "Inspector Gadget." It was an odd nickname for a man who in another compartment of his intellectual life had complained that modern man retreats "into the seductive tools and technologies of industrial civilization, but that only creates new problems."

Acting as the administration's chief shrink, Gore put psychologist/facilitator Jane Hopkins on the White House payroll to help his staff work on "group dynamics" and "relatedness." Early in the administration, Hopkins and Carolyn Lukenmeyer presided over a Camp David retreat at which President Clinton told about the pain of being a chubby child who got picked on by other children. Other cabinet members talked about their painful childhoods. Hopkins remained a part-time consultant on the White House payroll until Gore pushed the Democratic National Committee to hire her, at more than $3,000 per month, to advise him on staffing issues.

Gore understood that American politics had become a talk show of sorts, and if Clinton had seized the role of host, he was willing to play the guest psychologist. Having learned from Clinton that empathy is power, Gore wanted their administration to feel voters' pain. (Jack Germond and Jules Witcover wrote of attending a post-Columbine discussion between Gore and students on violence, which resembled "a group session with a psychiatrist.") Gore was instructing people on how to get on the road of well-being he had been traveling since the eruption of his midlife crisis.

It proved a smart bet for advisers to play to Gore's self-image as a philosopher-shrink. Writer Naomi Wolf wrote an article about Gore's "nerd-visionary instincts" and his "Blakean deep inside"—and wound up with a $15,000-per-month gig on the Gore 2000 campaign. Gore's daughter Karenna became a trusted adviser by flattering this aspect of Gore's self-image. When she was brainstorming with her father in preparation for his 1996 debate with Jack Kemp, Gore was searching for good football metaphors to launch at the former quarterback. If Kemp started making football analogies, Karenna suggested, "Dad, just tell him, 'Jack, if you keep talking about football, I'll have to give you a lecture about chlorofluorocarbons.'" Gore tried it, and got a laugh; more important, he was being amusing by reminding everyone of his intellectual superiority.

Then in September, Gore displayed his penchant for taking credit for other people's hard work when he held a press conference in Boston announcing $5 million in emergency aid for fishermen hurt by federal closures of fishing grounds in the Gulf of Maine. The fishermen thought that Gore was announcing extra aid in addition to the $5 million secured by Senator John Kerry (D-Mass.). Paul Cohane, head of the Gulf of Maine Fisherman's Association, told the Boston Globe, "It really stinks of cheap, election-year politics. Mr. Gore had very little to do with it, and yet he came and took all of the glory."

Gore reprised his role as the good son—part dutiful, part morally superior—during his years as Clinton's vice president. Just as young Gore had shown more scientific acumen than his father, the vice president was the science wonk within the administration, tackling technical issues that most politicos did not want to have to begin thinking about. Just as he unsuccessfully tried to scold his father into voting for the 1964 Civil Rights Act, he tried and failed to push Clinton to end discrimination against homosexuals in the military. And while press secretaries emphasized Gore's extreme loyalty and his refusal to undermine or upstage Clinton, the word nonetheless always managed to get out when Gore was considered to be on the "right" side of an issue, such as gay rights or U.S. intervention in Bosnia.

And just as Gore would put his father on a higher pedestal than Gore Sr. deserved, he also elevated Clinton beyond reason. Most notably, after the House voted to impeach Clinton in 1998, Gore led a pep rally on the White House lawn in which he proclaimed that Clinton would be considered "one of our greatest presidents."

By 1999, however, when Gore believed that Clinton's sins were hurting his chances for the White House, he became the rebellious son. Diane Sawyer asked him about the "greatest president" statement and noted, "You said that misleading statements are very different from lying. Is that the article of faith that you want to run your presidential campaign on?" To which he replied, "Well, no, of course not. That's in the context of the effort by—a partisan effort, what I felt was a partisan effort in the Congress to remove him from office." There was a dual message in his response. Gore had been forced by circumstances to support the president, and yet if he perceived something as partisan—and he invariably perceives any opposition as partisan—then he will fight as dirty as dirty can.

Perhaps the best description of Gore's ethical muddle comes from a piece that *Vanity Fair* editor Marjorie Williams wrote for the *Washington Post*:

> *Gore is not an insincere man; he is something potentially worse, a man who divorces his sincerity from his political actions, in the apparent belief that his morals are of no use in guiding him through a field that is all (to him) a moral quagmire. Gore has always seemed to think of himself as transcending the ordinary back-scratching of politics; he has a Lancelot air of knowing exactly where all of the limits are and of sternly, abstemiously observing them to the letter—right up until the moment when he feels he needs to bend one.*

In this passage, worth re-reading, Marjorie Williams has perfectly captured Al Gore, and the Gore Disconnect that defines his political personality.

CHAPTER TWO

The Enemy is Us

Republicans weren't the only ones to find fault with Gore's 1992 book *Earth in the Balance: Ecology and the Human Spirit*. Soon after it was published, a Democratic National Committee staffer named Jonathan Sallet wrote an internal memo entitled "Potential Attacks on 'Earth in the Balance.'" Covering himself by hailing the book as a "profile in courage" with a singular vision, Sallet wrote that he would deal with "technical objections" that could be made against the book in a later memo. For the time being, he wanted to go over some political and social statements that would be fodder for Republican critics.

He listed three themes of a likely attack. The first was: "Al is not qualified to be president." Sallet began, playing devil's advocate: "He has no principles. He admits that he has voted for programs in which he does not believe (EITB at 340), has changed his campaign tactics merely to suit the advice of political consultants (EITB at 8–9, at 167–169), and uses products that he simultaneously criticizes as being harmful to the environment." (Sallet was referring to Gore's admission that he used his car's air conditioning when driving to events where he advocated a ban on the chlorofluorocarbons that made air conditioning work.) The memo continued to probe the ways in which the book could affect perceptions of Gore's presidential qualifications. "He is a weak figure who, as he admits, feels 'paralyzed' (EITB at 2), who has suffered the throes of a mid-life crisis (EITB at 14), and who doesn't even know what he thinks (EITB at 13).... He is a hypocrite who urges population growth on others while revering his own large family (EITB at 307).... He is a bad scientist, who doesn't care enough to get his facts straight."

Moving to his second theme—"Al is a radical environmentalist who wants to change the very fabric of America"—Sallet wrote: "He criticizes America for being America—a place where people enjoy the benefits of an advanced standard of living (EITB at 147, 156, 161, 308).... He has no sense of proportion: He equates the failure to recycle aluminum cans with the Holocaust.... He is a Luddite who holds the naive view that technology is evil and wants to abolish automobiles (EITB at 206, 318).... He believes that our civilization, itself, is evil (because it is, in his words, 'addicted to the consumption of the earth') (EITB at 220)."

Then came the third theme: "If Al Gore has his way, we would give up America's jobs and destroy the economy." In this connection, Sallet wrote, "All he wants to do is to raise a host of taxes, including carbon taxes, pollution charges, a 'Virgin Materials Fee,' and a gasoline tax (EITB at 273, 348–49).... He is a big spender who thinks that we have to support the environmental programs of the entire world." Also, Gore "wants to destroy the U.S. automotive industry and a lot of jobs along with it," "favors the spotted owl over jobs" and "wants to give away American technology."

That's *Earth in the Balance* in a nutshell, although the friendly fire of Sallet's memo actually underplayed the extent to which this strange work reads like the Greatest Hits of the Apocalypse. Gore's book—which ironically solidified his reputation as a deep thinker—buys into virtually every scientific scare story about the modern world, and does so with a breathless near-hysteria suggested by the following excerpts (the italics are mine):

"We now know that [cars'] cumulative impact on the global environment is posing a mortal threat to the security of every nation that is *more deadly than that of any military enemy we are ever again likely to confront.*"

"Just as men tear tusks from elephants' heads in such quantity as to threaten the beast with extinction, we are ripping matter from its place in the earth in such volume as to *upset the balance between daylight and darkness.*"

"The massive clearing of tropical rain forests is, of course, an ecological catastrophe of the first magnitude, beside which the Dust Bowl pales in comparison—not least because the earth could at least recover from the latter in a few generations, whereas the damage from the former could last for *tens of millions of years.*"

"As we strip-mine the earth at a completely unsustainable rate, we are making it impossible for our children's children to have a standard of living even remotely similar to ours."

"In the lifetimes of people now living, we may experience a 'year without a winter.' ... [W]e are carelessly initiating climate changes that could well last for hundreds or thousands of years.... What if our children, because of our actions, face not a year without winter but a *decade without a winter?*"

Gore paid homage to the classic work of the eco-scare genre, Rachel Carson's *Silent Spring*, first published in 1962, and made it clear that he considered his own book to rest squarely in the prophetic tradition she established. Carson's role of Cassandra—superior to all, but heeded by none—was irresistible to

Gore. Yet as Gregg Easterbrook points out in his fine book *A Moment on the Earth*, "Nothing Carson forecast in *Silent Spring* came to pass." That's partly because governments, corporations and people modified their behavior in response to her warnings, of course, but it is also because pesticides weren't nearly as destructive as she contended they were. In any case, the eco-catastrophe she predicted was vastly oversold. She wrote that the robin was on the verge of extinction, for instance, yet the American robin population has grown each year since she wrote the book. In fact, of the forty birds whose extinction or near extinction she warned against, only seven have declined, while nineteen have remained stable and fourteen actually have increased their population—which, Easterbrook explains, "sounds like business as usual for nature."

Gore, like Carson, wrote of global catastrophe with hair-raising conviction. He exhibited no room for doubt, no respect for inconvenient facts, and no time for theories that did not forecast worldwide annihilation. He was certain that human-caused global warming is a fact, certain that it would bring about a host of disasters in short order, and certain that unless Americans followed his lead promptly, the earth soon would disintegrate.

The book was a bestseller, but for some it functioned more as a disturbing piece of autobiography than a work of science or social commentary. "If Gore is still even half the man he was when he wrote *Earth in the Balance*," Jonathan Rauch recently commented in *National Journal*, "then the prospect of a Gore presidency seems unsettling. Not because of what Gore says, or even what he does, but because of the sort of person he is. Hysterics don't belong in the Oval Office, or anywhere near it."

As vice president, he has continued to play the role of a latter-day Nostradamus. Whenever there is a weather trouble spot in the country, Gore seems to turn up to point out how the grim meteorology confirms his fear of imminent global overheating. If there's a heat wave, he's there with a worried I-told-you-so look on his face. Floods in the Midwest? Gore also has tied them to global warming. Wildfires in Florida? The culprit must be human-caused climate changes. While El Niño was drenching California, Gore told a crowd in Santa Monica, "We may look back at this as the turning point." After Hurricane Floyd had torn up the East Coast in 1999, he pointed out that scientists say hurricanes "could become stronger with the warming trends."

In a 1997 speech at Glacier National Park, Gore asserted, "The overwhelming evidence shows that global warming is no longer a theory—it's a reality." And if it isn't stopped, "Infectious diseases could spread, affecting families and children in regions that had been too cold for tropical viruses to survive. Farmers and rural communities could be in jeopardy, since farms depend on a stable climate to be productive.... Our seas could rise by one to three feet, flooding thousands of miles of Florida, Louisiana and other coastal areas."

Contrary to Gore's assertion, global warming is not a fact but a theory. It may be happening, it may not be. And if it is happening, industrial technology is responsible for only part of the increase in greenhouse gases. What's more, some scientists have suggested that even if human-induced global warming is occurring, it may have only modest, even benign, consequences, such as raising nighttime and winter temperatures, or only warming air around the two poles.

It is true that land temperatures have hit historic highs in the 1990s. NASA's Goddard Institute for Space Studies in New York found that 1990 was the hottest year since 1866, then 1995 beat the record again, then 1998 was hotter. But one factor in this rise may be that temperatures often are measured near population centers—known as "heat islands"—which naturally would tend to be hotter than less populated areas. Overmeasuring in the Northern Hemisphere and undermeasuring in the Southern Hemisphere may skew results further. It is also true that NASA detected a cooling trend in the atmosphere while it was measuring warmer land temperatures.

And for someone obsessed with global well-being, Gore seems to have only a shaky sense of geological time. He wrote that 1990 was the "warmest year on record." But as Gregg Easterbrook asks, "Compared to what? The 'record' goes back only to the 1880s, when systematic preservation of weather data began. It turns out that the late 1880s was a cold period. Earth could experience 'record' warmth relative to the 1880s and remain cool compared to the bulk of its past."

In *Earth in the Balance*, Gore framed the issue as one in which 98 percent of scientists agree that a crisis exists. He then excoriated the media for having the cheek occasionally to present both sides of the issue, suggesting that reporters should self-censor news from the dissenting side. If only 2 percent of scientists disagreed with Gore's position, as he claimed, this annoyance might make some sense. But a Gallup poll taken in 1992—the year *Earth in the Balance* was released—found that 53 percent of scientists involved in climate research did not believe human-induced global warming had occurred, 30 percent didn't know, and only 17 percent believed man had created global warming.

Gore's scientific mentor and global warming guru, the late Roger Revelle—his professor at Harvard and one of the first scientists to monitor and voice concern about the increase of carbon dioxide in the atmosphere—was one of those who expressed reservations. In 1988, Revelle wrote to Gore's buddy, then-Senator Tim Wirth (D-Co.),

> *I agree with your statement that "Global climate change may well be the most challenging environmental, economic and political issue we*

have ever faced." However, we must be careful not to arouse too much alarm until the rate and amount of warming becomes clearer. It is not yet obvious that this summer's hot weather and drought are the result of a global climatic change or simply an example of the uncertainties of climate variability. My own feeling is that we had better wait another ten years before making confident predictions. One reason for thinking so is that there is not much evidence for global ocean warming, and that must occur before there is a serious long-term change in the atmospheric climate.

Yet Gore sees no room for doubt, or for questions or caution. In fact, in *Earth in the Balance,* he likens global warming and ozone depletion to the circumstances leading up to the Holocaust. He writes, "Today the evidence of an ecological Kristallnacht is as clear as the sound of glass shattering in Berlin." He adds,

Minor shifts in policy, marginal adjustments in ongoing programs, moderate improvements in laws and regulations, rhetoric offered in lieu of genuine change—these are all forms of appeasement, designed to satisfy the public's desire to believe that sacrifice, struggle, and a wrenching transformation of society will not be necessary. The Chamberlains of this crisis carry not umbrellas but "floppy hats and sunglasses"—the palliative allegedly suggested by a former secretary of the interior as an appropriate response to the increased ultraviolet radiation caused by the thinning of the ozone layer.

In other words, being insufficiently sensitive about the environment is like beginning the Final Solution, and suggesting such palliatives as wearing sunscreen is tantamount to letting Hitler take over Czechoslovakia. Except that, according to Gore, it was easier to fight the Third Reich. In an astonishing display of vainglory, he writes, "The struggle to save the global environment is in one way much more difficult than the struggle to vanquish Hitler, for this time the war is with ourselves. *We are the enemy...*" (my italics).

A Disease of the Soul

Gore's position is close to one popularized by the cartoon character Pogo: "We have seen the enemy and he is us." Gore believes that "we" have created a "dysfunctional civilization" that separates us from the natural state we once enjoyed. Driven by a hunger incapable of satisfaction, a hunger that pushes people into "consuming larger and larger quantities every year of coal, oil, fresh air and water, trees, topsoil, and the thousand other substances we rip from the crust of the earth," modern man has become "addicted to the consumption of the earth itself."

If consumption is a crime, then America must be "the enemy" because it is the comfort capital of the world. According to Gore, that high quality of life is a disease of the soul. He says this in a way that leaves the strong implication that the era when man was ignorant, often half-starved, fearful of being eaten alive, unprotected from the elements and at the mercy of blind fortune was in reality a golden age. Americans overconsume, he explains, "not because we don't care but because we don't really live in our lives." The modish idea of "living in our lives," which sounds like a phrase from one of the human potential workshops he set up at the White House, is never really explored or explained.

At times Gore seems afflicted with what Freud might have called deprivation envy. He writes, "Just as children cannot reject their parents, each new generation in our civilization now feels utterly dependent on the civilization itself. The food on the supermarket shelves, the water in the faucets in our homes, the shelter and sustenance, the clothing and purposeful work, our entertainment, even our identity—all these our civilization provides, and we dare not even think about separating ourselves from such beneficence." Listening to the meanings behind these words, one understands why columnist Tony Snow in 1995 wrote an article highlighting likenesses in quotes from Gore's book and the manifesto of the yet-to-be-identified Unabomber.

Gore's book not only gave him the opportunity to demonstrate his moral superiority but also allowed him to show off the wonky Mr. Science side of his personality. In the conclusion, he writes about the "new theory called self-organized criticality" championed by Per Bak and Kan Chen of the Brookhaven National Laboratory. The two physicists watched each grain of sand as it was poured into a sand-pile to understand the critical point when an avalanche is triggered. Gore writes, "The sand-pile 'remembers' the impact of each grain that is dropped and stores that memory holistically (or holographically) in the physical position of all the grains in relation to one another and in the full three-dimensional shape of the pile itself. The sand-pile theory— self-organized criticality—is irresistible as a metaphor." As if in an elaborate illustration of the Gore Disconnect usually apparent only in the political arena, he writes yearningly in one chapter of the simpler days before supermarkets and plumbing, and in another chapter he revels in sand-pile theories hatched in well-equipped laboratories.

Gore also writes about the special pain of being an intellectual, a theme which controversial feminist adviser Naomi Wolf picked up on so aptly in her *George* magazine piece when she wrote about the psychic "toll" he no doubt paid for being both a savant and a senator's son. As Gore himself puts it, "Insisting on the supremacy of the neo-cortex exacts a high price, because the unnatural task of a disembodied mind is to somehow ignore the *intense psychic pain* that comes from the constant nagging awareness of what is missing: the experience of living in one's body as a fully integrated physical and mental being" (my italics).

Clinging to the psychobabble in Gore's writing is, however, an odor of misanthropy. In a piece for *Time* in 1989, he wrote, "Now the question is: Did God choose an appropriate technology when he gave human beings dominion over the earth? The jury is still out." He fine-tunes his anti-humanist critique so that it resonates with the feminist world view:

> *As the scientific and technological revolution has picked up speed, we have seemed to place a good deal more emphasis on technologies that extend and magnify abilities—such as fighting wars—historically associated more with males than females.... Ultimately, part of the solution for the environmental crisis may well lie in our ability to achieve a better balance between the sexes, leaving the dominant male perspective with a healthier respect for female ways of experiencing the world.*

But Gore's misanthropic streak, eerily close to the eco-extremism of groups like Earth First, ultimately trumps gender. Here is what he writes about a natural substance that can be particularly salutary for women's health:

> *The Pacific yew can be cut down and processed to produce a potent chemical, taxol, which offers some promise of curing certain forms of lung, breast, and ovarian cancer in patients who would otherwise quickly die. It seems an easy choice—sacrifice the tree for a human life—until one learns that three trees must be destroyed for each patient treated, that only specimens more than a hundred years old contain the potent chemical in the bark, and that there are very few of these yews remaining on earth. Suddenly we must confront some tough questions.*

Tough questions? What's tough about choosing a woman's life

over that of a tree? This odd passage not only shines a bright light on the true nature of Gore's environmentalism, but also raises questions about the medical policies he might pursue as president.

A Wrenching Transformation

Critics have not been unfair when they charge that Gore's environmentalism is extreme and would entail returning America to the technological dark ages. They merely have taken seriously what he wrote. In his *Time* essay, for instance, he warns that "many of the ultimate solutions are unimaginably difficult." In *Earth in the Balance,* he foresees a "wrenching transformation of society" that may entail a government mandate of "completely eliminating the internal combustion engine over, say, a 25-year period." His anti-car bent is clear as he writes, "Objectively, it makes little sense for each of us to burn up all the energy necessary to travel with several thousand pounds of metal wherever we go, but it is our failure to think strategically about transportation that has led to this absurd state of affairs."

At one point, Gore muses that even if there were a new "miraculous technology that enabled human civilization to cut per capita emissions of greenhouse gases in half," that would not be enough to prevent global warming, and "we will have to cut emissions even more than that." He proposes a pollution tax, or CO_2 tax, on gasoline, heating oil, coal, natural gas and electricity, but won't say how much. He says that he would reduce income taxes by the amount of his pollution tax, so that families wouldn't have to pay more taxes. In the next breath, however, he proposes using the new CO_2 tax revenue to pay for an Environmental Security Trust Fund that would subsidize hardship cases as well as the purchase of "benign technologies"—as in low-energy light bulbs and high-mileage cars. Gore also proposes a Virgin Materials Fee, which he again fails to quantify, that would increase the price of manufacturing goods made from "nonrenewable, virgin materials."

In the regulation department, Gore calls for higher mileage requirements for "all trucks and cars sold in the United States," an accelerated phase-out of ozone-destroying chemicals (which the Senate passed in 1995) and tougher efficiency standards for home appliances. Only once does he give so much as a hint of the price tag for his wrenching transformation—which he calls a Global Marshall Plan (a title suggesting that the brunt of this global initiative would be borne by the United States). He suggests that an appropriate figure would equal the annual U.S expenditures for the previous Marshall Plan between 1948 and 1951, which was close to 2 percent of our GNP. "A similar percentage today would be almost $100 billion a year (compared to our total nonmilitary foreign aid budget of about $15 billion a year)."

Then–Vice President Dan Quayle cited that passage in their 1992 debate and charged, "One of the proposals that Senator Gore has suggested is to have the taxpayers of America spend $100 billion a year on environmental projects in foreign countries…"

"That's not true," Gore cut in, as he had when Quayle brought up his record on abortion.

"Foreign aid," Quayle shot back. "Well, Senator, it's in your book. On page 304."

"No, it's not," Gore replied, as the Gore Disconnect kicked in. He added, "There's no such proposal."

Gore's Global Marshall Plan would combine "large-scale, long-term, carefully targeted financial aid to developing nations, massive efforts to design and then transfer to poor nations the new technologies needed for sustained economic progress, a worldwide program to stabilize world population, and binding commitments by the industrial nations to accelerate their own transition to an environmentally responsible pattern of life." It is not enough to share the very technologies that make the U.S. competitive with countries employing cheaper labor and create the wealth to be able to afford Marshall Plans; the United States—perhaps to atone for its affluence—also must forgive Third World debts. In return, grateful Third World countries— and Gore expects them to be grateful, despite many experiences to the contrary—would turn to Gore's America for leadership in the areas of social justice, human rights, adequate nutrition, health care, shelter, literacy and political freedom.

In a very real sense, Gore is advocating a type of global communism, where developed nations and their corporations would be forced to relinquish property rights, intellectual property and lifestyle comforts to less fortunate countries, which magically would be transformed by this infusion of reparations into havens of environmental sanity, good government, and civil rights. But because there is virtue in poverty, Gore actually expects these countries to behave better than the hyper-consuming bourgeoisie that has helped them out of their troubles.

Gore's Global Marshall Plan would be administered in part by a Strategic Environmental Initiative, a board designed to create and enforce "a new generation of environmental antitrust laws" that would scrutinize vertical integration of resources. He would make it illegal, say, for pesticide companies to buy up seed companies—lest they try to create seeds that require more pesticide use—or for large paper users to buy forest land. The SEI would "plant billions of trees" and establish a network of training centers to educate people around the world about the environment.

▲

Midway through *Earth in the Balance*, Gore recalls a 1989 hearing he held as a senator on global warming, which featured the testimony of Dr. James Hansen, a top NASA scientist. In this hearing, Hansen disclosed that someone from the Bush White House had pushed him to change his testimony and not describe global warming as "probable." He was referring to the fact that someone in the Office of Management and Budget had added two paragraphs to Hansen's remarks that were designed to mute his message. It was an improper act that muddied science with politics, and Gore legitimately was furious. He called the action "a form of scientific fraud" and told Hansen that if administration officials "attempt any kind of retribution in return for candor, they will have on their hands the congressional equivalent of World War III."

The irony is that Gore himself has been far from tolerant when dealing with scientists whose views diverge from his own. When Gore was still a senator, Jonathan H. Adler, environmental policy analyst for the Competitive Enterprise Institute, wrote that his "subcommittee hearings have become circuses where only those who agree with him are allowed to testify." The fate of William Happer Jr. is a cautionary tale about what happens when someone crosses Al Gore.

With the support of congressional Democrats, Happer, director of energy research at the Department of Energy under Bush, had been asked to stay on after Clinton was elected. In May 1993, he testified before Gore's committee, "As an individual, I think that there has been an exaggeration of the dangers of ozone depletion and climate change." He also cited a decline in the ultraviolet radiation hitting the earth's surface and questioned whether spy satellites should be used in ecological monitoring, which Gore had advocated successfully.

Those opinions conflicted directly with *Earth in the Balance*, where Gore warns that a thinning of the ozone layer decreases plants' ability to photosynthesize, increases cases of skin cancer and cataracts, and may have a connection with the discovery of blind rabbits and blind salmon in Patagonia. In 1992, when there were reports of an ozone hole in North America, Gore declared that it was "the greatest crisis humanity has ever faced." (The story turned out to be a bust. There is and was no ozone hole in the Northern Hemisphere. The *Washington Post* checked up on the reports of blind bunnies and fish, only to discover that these cases were caused by an outbreak of conjunctivitis.)

Within a month of his candid testimony, Happer was out of his job. The word on Capitol Hill was that Gore had arranged his termination. Said the late Congressman George Brown Jr., then-chairman of the House Committee on Science, Space, and Technology, "Happer marches to a different drummer than Al Gore. Will is a pure scientist. Al Gore is a politician." *Physics Today* wrote, "The sacking of Happer, a former Princeton University physics professor with impressive credentials, raises questions about whether the Administration will be able to recruit scientists for sensitive positions when science conflicts with politics."

In addition to William Happer, there's also the unhappy example of S. Fred Singer, a former professor of environmental sciences at the University of Virginia and one-time chief scientist at the U.S. Department of Transportation. In 1991, Singer co-wrote an article for the Cosmos Club journal, *Cosmos*—a small magazine for the 3,000-member Washington, D.C., social club—with Chauncey Starr and Gore's own Harvard mentor Roger Revelle, who died shortly after publication. The piece was aptly entitled "What to Do About Greenhouse Warming: Look Before You Leap." It stated, "The scientific base for a greenhouse warming is too uncertain to justify drastic action at this time. *There is little risk in delaying policy responses* to this century-old problem since there is every expectation that scientific understanding will be substantially improved within the next decade" (my italics).

It did not sit well with Gore that his esteemed professor—whom he had praised effusively in *Earth in the Balance*—espoused an opinion contrary to his own. After Gregg Easterbrook wrote a story critical of Gore in the *New Republic* citing the *Cosmos* article, Gore people waged a whispering campaign alleging that Singer had tricked Revelle into putting his name on the piece. Yet Gore should have been aware of Revelle's call for caution because of the letter Revelle had written to their mutual friend Senator Tim Wirth to that effect in 1988.

Anxious to find a way of explaining his revered mentor's apostasy, Senator Gore personally called a Harvard researcher close to Revelle, Dr. Justin Lancaster, and asked Lancaster about Revelle's "mental capacity" at the time the *Cosmos* article was written. Lancaster told Gore that Revelle was "mentally very sharp to the end." Gore nonetheless suggested that Lancaster write a sharp letter responding to the *New Republic* article. Lancaster wrote the letter, in which he suggested that Singer had prodded a "reluctant" Revelle into putting his name on the article.

Lancaster didn't stop there. On his own he tried to pressure the publisher planning on reprinting the Revelle/Singer/Starr article in an anthology to spike it. He wrote,

> *It should be known that Roger Revelle was not an author of this* Cosmos *article, which was misleading and unscholarly; nor did that paper represent Revelle's views. The chief author, S. Fred Singer, entered Revelle as a coauthor despite his objections. Subsequent to Revelle's death in 1991, Singer ambitiously distributed the article and has sought republication in a singular attempt to undermine the pro-Revelle stance of Senator Al Gore, Revelle's former student.*

Singer sued Lancaster for libel and won a settlement in 1994. As part of the settlement, Lancaster released a statement in which he retracted his "unwarranted" statements that said or implied "that Professor Revelle was not a true and voluntary author of the *Cosmos* article."

But Gore continued to cling to the fiction that Revelle didn't believe in a cautious approach to the issue of global warming. During the 1992 vice presidential debate, when Reform Party candidate Admiral James Stockdale said, "I read where Senator Gore's mentor disagreed with some of the scientific data that is in his book. How do you respond to those criticisms of that sort?" Gore answered that just before Roger Revelle died, "he co-authored an article which was—had statements taken completely out of context."

As vice president, Gore would not let the matter rest. Despite his own cozy relationship with Occidental Petroleum, he personally called *Nightline* in 1994 to suggest that the news show investigate the funding of Singer and other global warming critics. As Ted Koppel explained on air, "The vice president suggested that we look into connections between scientists who scoff at the so-called greenhouse effect, for example, and the coal industry." He added, "There was also a connection, he said, to the Reverend Sung Myung Moon's group." Koppel admitted that Gore's people had passed information about Singer's funding on to him.

The *Nightline* segment was fascinating. In his appearance, Singer didn't deny that he had received consulting fees from Exxon, Shell, Arco and Sun oil companies. He told Koppel that no one had ever directly accused him of being an industry mouthpiece, "but if that were to happen, I would simply point to the fact that every environmental organization I know of gets money from Exxon, Shell, Arco, Dow Chemical and so on."

Asked if the money he received had tainted his science,

Singer replied, "If it doesn't taint their science, it doesn't taint my science." Indeed, Singer was vindicated when Koppel showed footage from a 1991 *Nightline* on which he had appeared opposite Gore hero Carl Sagan. They were discussing the possible environmental effects of the oil fires that the Iraqis set in Kuwait during Desert Storm. Singer predicted that the smoke would not reach higher than three thousand feet, then rain out after three to five days. Sagan said the soot would hit a much higher altitude. Singer turned out to be right.

Having endured a lawsuit and smears on her husband's reputation, Singer's wife and colleague, Candace Crandall Singer, walked away from the nasty episode concluding this about Gore:

> *He seems to genuinely believe that his goals—whatever they are— are being thwarted by some vast industry-led conspiracy, and he keeps searching for someone, especially someone in the news media, who will uncover it for him....He appears to have a weakness for associating himself with people who are given to reckless behavior, and whose paranoia feeds his sense of being under siege. Again, not the kind of trait one would want to see in a national leader.*

CHAPTER THREE

Politics in the Balance

While writing *Earth in the Balance*, Al Gore had an epiphany. He realized that just as massive taxpayer subsidies pay for the construction of logging roads that lay waste to old forests, "the destruction of the Everglades is being actively subsidized by taxpayers and consumers through artificial price supports for sugarcane—a crop that otherwise would never be grown in that area."

In the past, Gore had voted for the subsidies, and voted against a measure—ironically offered by then-Senator Bill Bradley (D-N.J.)—to cut government price supports for sugar. Never again, Gore declared; "Change is possible: I, for one, have decided as I write this book that I can no longer vote in favor of sugarcane subsidies; looking beyond this particular case, I want to shift the burden of proof to the advocates of subsidies, to show that ecological problems will not occur as a result of distorting the market."

In his mea culpa, Gore does not mention the generous contributions Big Sugar made to his House and Senate campaigns. Those donations, however, were nothing compared to the industry's largesse once he and Clinton were in the White House. Sugar czar Alfonso Fanjul, his family, their company Flo-Sun Inc. and other corporate entities gave $204,500 to Democrats in the 1996 election cycle alone. And they got their money's worth. In the White House, Gore, like Clinton, has been once again a solid backer of Big Sugar, doling out federal corporate welfare for sugar growers in the form of price supports, import quotas, and federally guaranteed loans. The General Accounting Office believes federal import quotas alone cost U.S consumers more than $1 billion annually in the form of higher soft drink, candy and food prices. Thomas Schatz of Citizens Against Government Waste charged, "A handful of wealthy sugar cane barons, who represent less than one percent of the nation's sugar growers, gobble up 58 percent of the program benefits. These are not small family farmers. In a recent year, 33 cane sugar growers obtained more than $1 million each from this government boondoggle and one grower alone received $65 million."

The sugar giveaways may have cost workers their jobs as well. Since the federal government began bolstering Big Sugar in 1981, the *Reader's Digest* reports, twelve of the industry's twenty-two U.S. refineries have closed, due in part to the artificially inflated price of sugar purchased in the United States. Other refineries, like the C&H Sugar Co. of Crockett, California, have reduced their workforce substantially.

But the vice president has stuck by Big Sugar—despite its damage to the Everglades and the sugar programs' cost to consumers and taxpayers, and despite his dramatic pledge in *Earth in the Balance* and his later assertion to *Time* magazine, "There's not a statement in that book that I don't endorse. Not one. The evidence has firmed up the positions I sketched there."

▲

Given the Gore Disconnect, it should be no surprise that there is a significant difference between Al Gore in theory and Al Gore in practice. Of course it would be unrealistic to expect a politician with great expectations to push for the end of the combustion engine, even if he believed deeply in this cause. What has been surprising, however, is that when Gore has had golden opportunities to push for modest incremental changes in areas where he is supposedly most deeply committed, he has choked. After announcing that environmental ruination could destroy the planet and debase the lives of his own children and grandchildren, he hasn't jeopardized his own career to champion practical reforms that would be merely difficult, not impossible, to achieve. *Earth in the Balance* has served as a shallow and self-indulgent summoning of ideas that could be discarded as easily as they were once embraced whenever Gore found other causes—family leave, the V-chip, etc.—that would allow him to pose as the savior of the middle class.

It is not surprising, therefore, that Gore has not always been the Prince of Greenness. His cumulative League of Conservation Voters rating as a member of the House and Senate was 64 percent—far lower than the 84 percent garnered by, say, his one-time opponent Bill Bradley. Among other votes as a congressman, Gore has trespassed against environmentalism by voting to exempt a Tennessee Valley Authority dam from the Endangered Species Act, thus putting a pork-barrel project before the Little Tennessee River snail darter.

In one sense, Gore really is very much a farm boy at heart—not so much in the sense of working the land as in feeling entitled to federal subsidies. Federal subsidies were such an integral part of the Gore family ethos, after all, that the Gores grew federally subsidized tobacco while Nancy Gore Hunger had cancer and after she died. Even as Gore was writing a book that criticized Americans for being "addicted" to supermarket food and consuming the earth, his family was continuing in its long addiction to federal agriculture subsidies.

Gore has supported massive ethanol subsidies, which help corn farmers but have cost taxpayers more than $2.6 billion since 1996, and has even bragged that he made "a tie-breaking vote in the Senate to save it." (The vice president may argue that ethanol is good for the environment, but the General Accounting Office has found that the additive actually reduces automobile mileage by 3.6 percent.) He supported federal tobacco policies that fatten the purses of tobacco growers even as he ostensibly was trying to put tobacco out of business. As a senator he voted against reducing dairy price supports. Gore's position on corporate welfare for farmers is summed up by this campaign 2000 remark in Omaha: "We need to raise prices and lift exports."

Jonathan Adler of the Competitive Enterprise Institute explains, "When he's pro-environment, he always wants more regulations and more government programs. And when he's anti-environment, it's always in defense of a government program." Thus, as vice president, Gore announced that the administration was going to give $50 million to hog farmers. Running for president now, he supports even greater subsidies for farmers.

When Gore was running for president in 1988, he reversed a long campaign he had waged to get the Environmental Protection Agency to clamp down on water pollution from a North Carolina mill owned by International Champion Corporation, which dumped waste that ran into the Pigeon River in Tennessee. When it became clear to Gore that he could not win the support of local political leaders crucial for victory in North Carolina, he suddenly advocated a more balanced, less regulatory approach. Environmentalists felt betrayed. Yet, in light of Gore's environmental record in the House and Senate, they probably shouldn't have been shocked.

As vice president, Gore angered environmentalists when, as part of his Reinventing Government effort, he helped to put Elk Hills, 47,000 acres of oil-rich publicly owned land held by the U.S. Navy, on the auction bloc. In 1997, Armand Hammer's old company, Occidental, won a competitive bid by paying $3.65 billion for the rights to Elk Hills.

Throughout his career, Gore, like his father before him, has been an avid backer of the FDR-created taxpayer-subsidized pork-barrel Tennessee Valley Authority (TVA), despite its many coal-fired generating stations and three nuclear power plants, and despite the fact that the TVA represents the sort of energy policy any committed environmentalist ought to oppose because it sells its product too cheaply, thereby encouraging profligate energy use.

William Niskanen, a member of Ronald Reagan's Council of Economic Advisors in 1982, found out first-hand just how pro-tective Gore could be of the TVA. After the Council had met to dis-cuss market pricing for public utilities, a reform that would increase energy prices for consumers of the heavily subsidized TVA, Representative Gore personally called Niskanen and invited him to discuss the issues with him and some other members of Congress. Niskanen agreed. He asked Gore if he should bring charts or aides. Gore said it wasn't necessary, leaving Niskanen with the impression it would be an informal briefing.

An hour before his appearance, Gore's secretary called to tell Niskanen that the location of the meeting had been changed to a House committee room. When Niskanen entered he found a dozen members of Congress from the Tennessee Valley and the Pacific Northwest, where energy is heavily subsidized. There were television cameras from the members' home districts, along with some angry constituents. It was in October, just weeks before the 1982 elections: an opportune moment for members to harangue Niskanen, on camera, for wanting to take bread out of widows' mouths. And they did.

"On reflection, I thought that I was naive. I took Gore at his word," Niskanen later recalled. He believed he had been blindsided for taking a good-government position. A colleague quipped that Niskanen "had been gored."

Earth Summitry

In *Earth in the Balance,* Gore excoriated President Bush for his "disastrous and immoral" policy on global warming, and criticized him for relying on "symbolic actions." In 1992, Senator Al Gore complained that President Bush had embarrassed the nation at the Rio de Janeiro Earth Summit by refusing to sign an international biodiversity treaty as well as a greenhouse gas treaty.

Yet as Gregg Easterbrook writes in *A Moment on the Earth*—which could be considered something of an anti–*Earth in the Balance*—"There is something faintly indecent about the world's heads of state gathering, as they did at Rio, to bestow many tens of billions of dollars on the greenhouse effect, a speculative concern, while not lifting a finger to assist 7.8 million children dead each year from drinking infected water and breathing dense smoke." Vice President Dan Quayle was more concerned about Gore's America-bashing. "You can spend all day explaining to some people that America has the world's best environmental record," Quayle noted, "yet they go to a foreign country like Brazil to bash America."

After their 1992 win, Gore argued that Clinton should agree to the Rio goal of reducing greenhouse gases to 1990 levels by the year 2000. (The Senate had voted to ratify the Rio treaty in 1992.) Treasury Secretary Lloyd Bentsen differed with Gore, and Energy Secretary Hazel O'Leary argued that there should be a study first to measure the effect on the U.S. economy. Gore said that agreeing to the Rio goals would send a message that the Clinton administration would be different from that of Bush. Gore won the debate.

73

On the first Earth Day he was in office, President Clinton pledged to reduce U.S. greenhouse gases to 1990 levels by the year 2000 and also announced that he would sign the Rio biodiversity treaty. The details would be worked out later. In the end, Clinton adopted Bush's voluntary approach, so abhorrent to Gore and the enviros when Bush was president, which relied on financial incentives to clean the environment.

What's more, for all Gore's railing against purely symbolic actions by Bush, the new administration caved early on two measures without which it would be impossible to meet the Rio goal. One was Clinton's proposal—in keeping with Gore's views in *Earth in the Balance*—for a broad-based $72 billion energy tax on most forms of energy sources, including coal, utilities and gasoline, based on the number of British Thermal Units they produce. The idea was to tax energy as a means to reduce consumption, thus reducing air pollution.

The problem is that the administration's BTU tax would have cost the average family an estimated $204 annually—despite candidate Clinton's pledge to reduce taxes for the middle class. Industry hated the tax; so did members of Congress on both sides of the aisle. In the end the BTU tax was, as one Democrat congressman put it, "emasculated." Washington agreed to a 4.3-cents-per-gallon increase of the gasoline tax (already at 14.1 cents per gallon), which raised some $23 billion, with Gore proudly casting the deciding vote while presiding over the Senate. The greens considered the outcome a loss: the tax increase was too small, and demand too inelastic, to reduce consumption noticeably. And after all Gore's bashing of Bush for not doing enough to clean up the environment, U.S. emissions in 1998 were 10.3 percent above 1990 levels, according to the Worldwatch Institute.

It also would have been impossible to meet the Rio goals without drastically reducing gasoline consumption, but the administration—in an area Clinton largely had ceded to Gore—

hasn't lifted a finger to increase fuel efficiency. While running for the White House, Clinton and Gore pledged to increase the fleet average for automobile fuel efficiency to 40–45 miles per gallon. But once elected, they failed to raise the standards from a fleet average of 27.5 miles per gallon set in 1988. The fact is that automotive fuel efficiency was greater when Ronald Reagan was president—and technology was twenty years younger—than it has been under Clinton/Gore.

The administration that signed the Rio treaty actually allowed America's overall automobile fuel efficiency to decline, as demand for light trucks, sport utility vehicles and minivans drove down America's miles per gallon. Call it the Yuppie Exemption, a gift to the growing number of affluent buyers of gas-guzzling SUVs, which account for almost half of new vehicles purchased. Despite protests from environmentalists, the administration failed to hold SUVs to the same standard as cars. This failure made no sense: If it is in the national interest to set fuel standards for passenger cars, why exempt half of all new vehicles? The answer is that the administration wasn't willing to separate middle class voters from their SUVs.

Some administration boosters blamed Republicans in Congress for the problem. But the administration could have changed the fleet standards before the GOP took over the House or later sent strong signals to the Republican leadership that tougher standards were non-negotiable. It failed to do so. According to *Newsweek*, the SUV discrepancy has raised oil consumption by almost a million barrels of oil each day and increased greenhouse gas emissions by 187 million tons per year. The administration's failure to improve fuel standards has exacerbated air pollution, which, unlike global warming, is a real, known and immediate health threat.

But as a candidate for president in 2000, after not only failing utterly to deliver on his campaign fuel-efficiency promises but also overseeing a decline in fuel efficiency, Gore once again began talking about pushing federal CAFE (corporate average fuel economy) standards up to 60 miles per gallon. The vice president knows that an affordable family-sized car that gets 60 mpg isn't feasible in the near future, and if it were, it would be wildly unpopular. (As a Ford spokesman noted, "When you talk about a 45 mpg CAFE, you're talking about putting most of America in cars smaller than an Escort, and right now those kinds of cars represent less than one percent in the United States. People don't want to buy them.") But candidate Gore, having failed to deliver on 40–45 mpg when he had a chance, now promises 60 miles per gallon.

▲

The Clinton/Gore attitude toward the Big Three automakers has been similar to its attitude toward Big Sugar. In September 1993, the administration announced the Partnership for a New Generation of Vehicles to develop an affordable family car that runs on 80 miles per gallon. To date, the federal government has spent some $1.5 billion of taxpayer money to help Daimler Chrysler, Ford, and General Motors, working with federal scientists, to develop what they call the Supercar, the car only Washington could build.

The Supercar is part of what Gore described in a 1999 piece for *Newsweek* as "A Third Way." The third way, in the economics of Goredom, is the public/private partnership. Under the Third Way, the government doesn't tell the Big Three: Make cars that consume less gasoline, reduce your fleet mpg average to 35 miles. No, the administration says: We'll give you millions of dollars of other people's money to work toward a goal that is almost three times tougher than the current standard, and somehow expect you to reach it without increasing the cost of the family car. And since there is an understanding—dubbed the Partnership for a

New Generation of Vehicles (PNGV)—that we want to be pals, in the meantime we, the government, will let you sell vehicles, like SUVs, that we consider wildly inefficient. In return, you won't bash us if we do some little thing you don't like.

Some would call the Supercar a visionary goal, a way to make the seemingly unachievable happen some day. Others would point out that this approach is exceedingly expensive and it shuns incremental reforms that can be implemented fairly painlessly in favor of more glamorous measures that may not come to fruition for decades. ("Tripling the fuel economy [of the average car] without sacrificing price or passenger comfort will be harder than putting a man on the moon," Commerce Department evaluator Robert Chapman once explained to the *Houston Chronicle*.)

But one thing is certain: The PNGV definitely has brought the Big Three closer to Gore. GM president Jack Smith helped him save face by saying that he foresaw the end of the internal combustion engine and that only a switch to diesel fuel could extend its life. This statement made Gore seem less of a nut for writing in favor of "completely eliminating the internal combustion engine over, say, a 25-year period."

In a reissue of *Earth in the Balance* for the year 2000, Gore wrote that he was "proud" to have called for an end to the combustion engine in twenty-five years. When asked in New Hampshire before its 2000 primary if he stood by this proposal, he cited industry support as he replied, "I think we can do it quicker. And I think the Big Three automakers are going to do it quicker than that." Within months, however, GM would recall its electric car, the EV1, because it was such a severe fire hazard that owners were urged to have tow trucks pick up their vehicles. At the time, only 450 of the 1,000 vehicles sold since its 1996 debut were still operational.

No fan of the big-ticket PNGV program, Ralph Nader

testified before the House Budget Committee, "It is hard to imagine an industry less in need of government support for research than the highly capitalized auto industry, which is reporting record profits year after year." The Sierra Club's Carl Pope is no fan of the program either. "We don't see the commitment from the auto industry. If PNGV had been tied to a firm commitment to get CAFE standards to 60 mpg, that would have been one thing, but PNGV has been from our point of view an irrelevancy."

An expensive irrelevancy at that. Honda, Toyota and Volkswagen have introduced cars that get around 70 miles per gallon—without any government money. While Detroit's Big Three introduce prototypes, Honda, Toyota and Volkswagen's cars are already on the market.

To assuage environmental groups and keep them from complaining too loudly, the administration made sure that greens got a cut of taxpayer money as well. In 1998, James M. Sheehan of the libertarian Competitive Enterprise Institute wrote a paper that listed $30 million in "greenhouse pork" which the EPA had awarded to advocacy groups, in accordance with Rio and other global green treaties, over a five-year period. This green log-rolling has allowed the administration to finance dire warnings about global warming and to leave environmentalists hoping that future politicians will do something about the problem.

Blowing Smoke

After Gore failed to push for carbon dioxide emission cuts in cars and power plants, Eric Olsen of the Natural Resources Defense Council told the *Washington Post* in 1994, "The administration takes strong stands on some environmental issues, but they are not really fighting for their positions." In *Earth in the Balance*, Gore wrote against logging on national forests: "This enormous taxpayer subsidy for the deforestation of public land contributes to both the budget deficit and ecological tragedy." The administration did reduce logging on public lands dramatically, announcing in 1993 that it would end logging subsidies in 62 of its 156 national forests. Still, the remainder of the boondoggle was sufficiently expensive for the Forest Service to admit that timber sales in national forests cost taxpayers more than $88 million in 1997.

In his book, Gore also denounced federal grazing policies that allow livestock to graze on the public dime and an 1872 federal law that allows mining companies to harvest publicly-owned minerals without really paying for them. The Clinton administration took aim at those giveaways in 1993 when Interior Secretary Bruce Babbitt had a plan to charge grazing fees for livestock on public lands. The administration also planned to charge a modest royalty, 12.5 percent, on gold, silver and other metals mined on federal lands.

It presented a golden moment, a cause that united environmentalists and those conservatives who oppose corporate welfare. But Clinton/Gore caved in within about a month of making the proposal. Michael Francis of the Wilderness Society complained, "I don't think I've ever seen a white flag get up so fast. The Clinton White House came out charging, but once close enough to see the whites of the enemies' eyes, turned tail." After the capitulation, according to sources in the Sierra Club, Gore told enviros, "Remember, I'm just the vice president."

This excuse didn't help him with all environmental groups. When the Friends of the Earth Political Action Committee endorsed Bill Bradley in 1999, the group's spokesman explained, "We had very high hopes for Al Gore, and we've been disappointed. He's talked the talk but he has simply been unable to walk the walk."

The question remains: Would Gore, freed from the con-
straints of the vice presidency, be more of an environmental president than Bill Clinton?

On the one hand, former Gore strategist Ray Strother told
TV commentator John McLaughlin, "I think when we're talking
about him being liberal, we're talking about the environment.
Yes, he's more liberal on the environment. And, yes, I think he'll
be a great deal more extreme on the environment." Paul Rauber
wrote in the Sierra Club's magazine, "Indeed, many environmentalists have endured the indignities and disappointments of the
Clinton era happy in the belief that Gore's turn is next, that someone who shares our sense of urgency about healing the earth
would soon have the power to turn his ideals into action."

On the other hand, there are a number of environmentalists still bitter at Gore's desertion of the cause. Gore had gone
from advocating an end to the combustion engine to toasting Chinese Premier Li Peng to seal a deal in which China bought five
Boeing jets and 100,000 Buicks and other GM cars. In 1997, when
enviros were criticizing the administration, Gore told the *New
York Times*, "Everybody knows my views. But I am not going to
publicly try to back the president in a corner. I have never done
that, and I never will."

Time magazine reported on a meeting in August 1998
between Gore and the heads of leading environmental groups
who wanted him to sign onto various options to cut CO_2 emissions from cars and coal-fired power plants in order to meet the
Kyoto environmental accords. They told Gore that no matter how
tough it would be, he should show leadership in support of their
plans. "The room grew suddenly frosty," *Time* wrote, "and Gore,
who in previous months had been speaking out on climate
change and fighting internally for more antipollution funding
said, 'Name a senator who would support me.' He then gave a lecture on global warming's vexing politics—the Senate would

soundly reject the treaty in its current form—and abruptly ended the meeting."

Gore later explained, "We lost the fight in 1993 [for a BTU tax]. Losing on impractical proposals that are completely out of tune with what is achievable does not necessarily advance your cause at all."

On the campaign trail in 1999, a very Clintonized Gore lectured an environmentalist who wanted to increase fuel taxes, "I don't favor increasing gasoline taxes or fuel taxes. That is not achievable. It does not build coalitions. It destroys coalitions."

The message: Gore is likely to stand up for environmental regulations—unless they block his climb up the political ladder.

The Road to Kyoto

Gore may be soft on Big Sugar and the Big Three automakers, the administration may have dropped the ball with the BTU tax and CAFE standards, but he remains jealous of his patent on the cause of global warming. This cause is his line in the sand. He wrote a book about it, and he's not about to announce that maybe he was wrong. So when he showed up at the United Nations Framework Convention on Climate Change in Kyoto, Japan, in December 1997, he moved quickly to put his signature on his signature issue.

At the time Gore left for Japan, Europeans were calling for a treaty that mandated a 15 percent reduction in emissions in the year 2010 from their 1990 level, but Clinton wanted to stabilize emissions at their 1990 level and the administration maintained it would not budge. By the time Gore landed in Japan, however, the administration had agreed to a 2–3 percent reduction.

Conference attendees had wanted to exempt developing nations, including China, India, and Saudi Arabia, from any limitations whatsoever. But Clinton had insisted that a Kyoto treaty should hold developing nations to some standard. The U.S. Senate wasn't about to countenance an agreement that would put American industry at a distinct competitive disadvantage, and months before the conference had voted 95–0 in favor of a resolution stating that the U.S. should not sign a treaty that exempted developing nations.

When Gore arrived in Kyoto, he repeated that the United States was willing to walk away rather than compromise on this key issue. But then he got Kyoto Fever and made a surprise announcement: "After talking with our negotiators this morning and after speaking on the telephone from here a short time ago with President Clinton, I am instructing our delegation right now to show increased negotiating flexibility if a comprehensive plan can be put in place, one with realistic targets and timetables, market mechanisms and the meaningful participation of key developing countries."

In the end, the administration gave a pass to China, which produces 13 percent of the world's greenhouse gases, and to more than 130 other countries, including India, Pakistan, Brazil, Saudi Arabia, Indonesia and Mexico.

The United States agreed to reduce greenhouse gas emissions to 93 percent of America's 1990 level by the years 2008 to 2012. In effect, this means reducing U.S. emissions by 30 percent below what they otherwise would be expected to be in a decade. The European Union agreed to an 8 percent reduction from 1990 levels, while Japan agreed to a 6 percent reduction. Russia and New Zealand agreed to stabilize their emissions at 1990 levels. Worldwide the pact called for a decrease of emissions by 5.2 percent of 1990 levels.

Gore persuaded Kyoto to agree to pollution credits, also called emissions trading, which might allow countries that have reduced their emissions to sell their remaining "pollution credits" to a country struggling to comply. If Gore deserves blame for agreeing to exempt developing countries—and he does—he also deserves credit for pushing for a market-oriented method of reducing greenhouse gases. It was this provision that later prompted India to sign a statement agreeing to cooperate with the U.S. in efforts to make Kyoto work.

"The imperative here is to do what we promise, rather than to promise what we cannot do," Gore told Kyoto.

Yet these were odd words from the partner in the Clinton Rio plan, which promised that industrial emissions in 2000 would equal those of 1990, when in 1997 they were actually running some 10 percent higher. And later, when he was a presidential candidate, it would be odd too for Gore to promise that one of his first presidential acts would be to ratify Kyoto, although it requires two-thirds approval in the Senate, which had already voted 95–0 against terms to which he agreed.

Wharton Econometric Forecasting Associates figured the cost of Kyoto could be more than $2,000 per household, could nearly double energy and electricity prices, and could raise gasoline prices by as much as sixty-five cents per gallon. The Clinton administration had admitted that simply stabilizing emissions could cost 900,000 jobs. After Gore's crumbling on something as modest as the BTU tax, it is impossible to imagine that as president he would push for Senate ratification of a treaty like Kyoto. It is very easy to imagine him merely playing lip service to the pact.

▲

While Kyoto allowed Gore to rehabilitate his persona as world savior, the effect was short-lived. As a member of an administration forced to negotiate tumultuous rapids—giving big agribusiness and chemical companies sweet treatment on pesticide regulation, for example—Gore, too, frequently had a hand in compromises that disillusioned the often overly demanding enviro lobbies.

In the years since *Earth in the Balance,* Gore's record has become a very muddy shade of green. Gore had proclaimed in his book that saving the environment should be "the central organizing principle for civilization." But in the spring of 1999, Gore's campaign web site listed his four priorities for America as education, faith-based organizations, prosperity and fighting cancer. The environment didn't even make the list. In his book, Gore writes that people will have to radically change their way of thinking and living—submit to a "wrenching transformation"— in order to save the planet. By 1997, he was saying, "My purpose is not to be alarmist—nor is it to say that we need radical changes in the way we live and work."

Off-shore drilling provided an example of backtracking in action. In 1992, Candidate Gore had told Florida voters, "George Bush pledged when he was running for office four years ago to protect the coast of Florida from off-shore drilling, and he broke that promise to Florida just like he broke his promise when he said, 'Read my lips.'" Aides explained to the *Los Angeles Times* that Bush had gone back on a campaign promise to include an eight-year drilling moratorium in an energy bill. Gore made it be known that Bill Clinton and he would never allow drilling off the coast of Florida.

In 1999, it was Gore who was equivocating about off-shore oil drilling on the Florida coast. As Commerce Secretary Bill Daley was holding hearings on a drilling project proposed by Chevron, aides told the *St. Petersburg Times* that Gore could not comment under the law. The decision put him to the right of Texas Governor George Bush and Florida Governor Jeb Bush, who both opposed the proposed project.

After Bill Bradley had won the endorsement of Friends of the Earth and Gore realized that he would have to fight for green support, he changed his tune on Florida drilling again. Gore 2000 produced an ad in which the candidate promised a moratorium on oil drilling leases off the coasts of California and Florida, including new drilling based on existing leases. Gore told reporters he also opposed drilling in waters off any states where residents oppose it. "For me this issue is not only an economic issue and a health issue," Gore explained. "It's also a moral issue."

A moral issue? Then why not ban new drilling off all the Gulf Coast states—not just Florida, but also Alabama, Louisiana, Mississippi and Texas? Those states, Gore told the *Houston Chronicle*, "have wanted different approaches and I have honored their desire for a different approach." So it's a moral issue only where it's unpopular; otherwise, it's an issue of popular sovereignty.

At one point in the primary season GOP political consultant Dan Schnur quipped, "It's amazing what a couple of good polls for Bill Bradley will do. Until three weeks ago, Al Gore was a new Democrat. Now all of a sudden, it's the AFL-CIO, the Rainbow Coalition and the save-the-whales crowd." Indeed, the vice president even hinted to the Associated Press that he had pushed Clinton to ban drilling off California and Florida permanently, but that he couldn't elaborate on that conversation because "I don't talk about my private arguments."

Meanwhile, when environmentalists pointed out that the Clinton administration could enact Gore's ban—and torpedo Chevron's drilling plans—right away, Gore explained that this would be wrong because, "Sometimes it takes a campaign and a dialogue with voters, where you put a bold proposal out there and endorse it before you have a mandate to do it."

It's almost as if Gore believes he is so noble for going out on a limb in calling for environmental reforms that he doesn't think he should have to go out on a limb to implement them. Call it win-win-win environmentalism. He makes wild proposals, like calling for an end to the combustion engine by 2017. But he never has to pay a political price, because he will claim that politics is, after all, the art of the doable. This allows him to tease the environmentalists into continuing the mutual flirtation as he tells them that he wants to do more. But if he wins the admiration of environmentalists for speaking boldly, he also courts the gratitude of industrialists for not acting boldly. And he does all this without having to surrender his self-righteous claim to being morally different from and superior to other politicians.

In 1992, when President Bush announced that the United States would accelerate its phase-out of ozone-depleting CFCs, and ban manufacture sooner than it would have to under an internationally negotiated phase-out schedule, Gore, who had called the ozone hole "the greatest crisis humanity has ever faced," should have applauded the decision. Instead, he sniffed that Bush's move was not enough, "His deadline is welcome, but still inadequate."

Then, after he and Clinton were elected, the greatest crisis wasn't so great any more. In 1993, DuPont, a one-time major manufacturer of the CFCs believed to cause ozone thinning, announced that it would stop producing CFCs in 1994, a year ahead of the Bush administration's speeded up, drop-dead date. The Clinton White House, however, didn't want DuPont to stop making CFCs ahead of schedule, because car owners whose air conditioning failed would have to rip out their old system and pay some $1,000 to fix it, which could hurt Clinton/Gore in their 1996 re-election bid. In fact, the White House told DuPont that if the company stopped making CFCs, the administration would give its manufacturing allowance to a rival company.

When enviros criticized Gore for this bizarre about-face, he complained to the *Boston Globe*, "That is a completely phony rap. I will accept the observation that there is some irony in this administration saying, you know, steady as you go," but a faster phase-out could create "chaos in the marketplace" and "undermine public support for the most rapid possible phase-out."

Gregg Easterbrook reported the following exchange:

Edgar Bronfman Sr., a member of the DuPont board, called Gore. Bronfman is an important donor to Democratic Party causes, someone the Clinton White House would be expected to treat deferentially. The conversation went poorly. The company made a major commitment to abolishing CFCs, *Bronfman is said by informed sources to have told Gore.* Why are we suddenly supposed to keep going? *"It's necessary," is the only answer Gore is said to have given.* So is this stuff really dangerous or not? *Bronfman pressed.* "All I can say is that it's necessary," *Gore replied. The call ended with Gore brusquely declaring he didn't want to talk about it any longer.*

CHAPTER FOUR

Goretopia

Once he had used *Earth in the Balance* to establish his laurels as a philosopher/politician capable of deep thinking and moral fervor, Gore's Disconnect allowed him to push some of the apocalyptic ideas in his book out of mind and then out of sight. In fact, he began his presidential campaign with a brand-new green issue—light green—that didn't even rate mention in the index of *Earth in the Balance:* sprawl. Gore had hopped onto the "smart growth" bandwagon alongside those who call themselves New Urbanists. Their goal—and now Gore's—is to increase "livability," which they argue has been undermined by suburban sprawl. New Urbanists advocate more public transit and less road construction, and denser development closer to cities. They also want to bring people together and improve the quality of life by creating more parks and sidewalks while losing less open space to development. These amenities, Gore and his fellow New Urbanists say, will increase American families' sense of community.

It is small wonder that Gore has adopted this issue as his own. Livability may not be as sexy a topic as the death of the biosphere, but it's closer to people's lives and a lot less scary. Sprawl—

and the suburban angst it symbolizes—provides Gore with a way to appeal to a large, affluent voting bloc: the 138 million people who live in America's suburbs. (As *Congressional Quarterly* reported, the number of suburban congressional districts rose from 88 to 160 between 1973 and 1996.) Al From, president of the moderate Democratic Leadership Council, praised Gore for putting "sprawl front and center as he prepares to pursue the presidency" and for offering a Democratic agenda to a group that often has tended to vote Republican. President Clinton, in an amusing Freudian slip during his 2000 State of the Union speech, praised Gore's sprawl agenda as "a new effort to make communities *more liberal*"—before correcting himself with the word "livable."

Gore's approach to the issue has enough urgency that it might actually might be called "Suburbs in the Balance." The vice president explained the problem in his seminal 1998 livability speech before the Brookings Institution in these terms: "Acre upon acre of asphalt have transformed what were once mountainous clearings and congenial villages into little more than massive parking lots. The ill-thought-out sprawl hastily developed around our nation's cities has turned what used to be friendly, easy suburbs into lonely cul-de-sacs"—to the New Urbanist, cul-de-sacs, like strip malls and parking lots, are intrinsically sinister—"so distant from the city center that if a family wants to buy an affordable home they have to drive so far that a parent gets home too late to read a bedtime story."

Gore says he has the key to improve these lives of quiet desperation. In the foreword to the administration's 1999 "Building Livable Communities" report, he explained,

> *In cities, suburbs, and small rural towns, citizens and community leaders are seeking new, better ways to grow. They share a vision of*

livable communities where working families have a little extra to invest in a college education, instead of sinking thousands of dollars a year into extra commuting costs. Where people leaving welfare eager to work have a way to get to their new jobs, and still pick up their children at day care. Where scarce resources are invested in existing neighborhoods instead of being siphoned away to help pave over farmland for new, ever more distant subdivisions. Where air and water quality go up, and taxes don't.

The vice president gave an even rosier preview of Goretopia when he said,

How do we build more livable communities? Places where families can walk, bike, shop and play together. Where people spend less time in traffic, and more time with family and friends. Where we restore historic neighborhoods; protect centuries-old farmland; turn shopping malls into village squares; and build parks, not just parking lots. By meeting these challenges, we can build an America that is not just better off, but better.

There is an irony in this vision for the future: it bears an uncanny resemblance to the 1950s, which for liberals always has been the Dark Decade. People like Al Gore traditionally have ridiculed conservatives for wanting to return to an era when families were more like the Cleavers in *Leave It To Beaver*. Yet Goretopia promises Norman Rockwell communities and village squares from a small-town time before chain stores, when high school students rode bikes and didn't drive cars, when commutes were short and vast subdivisions were unknown. Gore only departs from the organic wholesomeness of the 1950s by injecting the element of government-controlled planning. Goretopia is the ideal planned community of *The Truman Show*—an experiment in happiness controlled with godlike expertise from above.

Suburban Renewal

It is easy to see the appeal of the livability agenda. As suburbs get more crowded, many long-time suburbanites have come to believe there are too many other people in the suburbs. As rising property values make it impossible for young families to buy a home within an easy commute to work, they move to new subdivisions further away from the city, then they crowd the roads. The commute gets worse and people notice there are too many *other* people on the roads, just as there are too many *others* at the malls and other public places.

That's the angst that drives suburbanites to search for more serenity. And they are so frustrated in this search that they fall into the embrace of the New Urbanists, planners who are driven by the belief that too much affluence, not too little serenity, is the problem. Progressive Policy Institute senior fellow Fred Siegel, who takes issue with some of the New Urbanist snobbery, reminds us that before we condemn sprawl we should remember that it is "an expression of the upward mobility and growth in home ownership generated by our past half century of economic success."

It has long been an established practice amongst elites to bash the suburbs. Long established, that is, since the suburbs changed from being enclaves of the rich—like Philadelphia's Main Line or shi-shi parts of Long Island—to the Levittowns that offer a more affordable version of suburbia to the upwardly mobile. Gore shares this disdain for a benighted America where "thickets of strip development distort the landscape." And he counts on the fact that many suburbanites are now distraught enough to agree with him in embracing the New Urbanism agenda. Writing in *Parade* magazine, Dennis McCafferty summed up the appeal of having the government go after sprawl: "Many of us—or maybe I should say some part of most of us—are dismayed by the landscape and traffic that our own dollars and desires have wrought. That's why it is possible both to deplore the arrival of a new Home Deport in my area and also to shop there."

There are, of course, real problems in the suburbs. Traffic congestion creates pollution and, in certain areas, eats up an even bigger bite of busy people's time. Development creeps even further from the rich drama of the inner city. Many burghs have so little idiosyncratic character that you can drive down any large street, it sometimes seems, and see a strip mall with a Taco Bell, a big mall with a Target and an apartment complex and feel that you are in Anywhere (or Nowhere) U.S.A. In most of the rest of the world, of course, people pray for such problems. Still, many of these material changes in this very material world take away some of the joy and beauty in Americans' otherwise enviable lives.

But Gore's livability agenda is calculated to show that he feels this pain rather than to bring relief or improvement. His comrades in the New Urbanist movement want to draw lines around metropolitan areas, prohibit development outside those areas, and increase development within city limits. They say they want more transportation choices—which is their disingenuous way of saying they want to starve road construction budgets in order to force more people onto public transportation. They would dump more transportation dollars into public transit systems and technologies that are supposed to ease congestion. They advocate denser communities—that is, smaller homes closer together and closer to the city. They promise less driving and more infill development (urban redevelopment on top of urban blight). They want to redistribute wealth by transferring public and private enterprises to the inner city.

Thus the New Urbanist agenda unites two causes dear to the

left: environmentalism and redistributionism. Advocates for both causes unite in their condemnation of big homes and big yards and the big family car. They unite in their desire to drive people into urban areas, enforcing "diversity" and preventing families from living in the seclusion they have redefined as "alienation."

As one New Urbanist developer told *U.S. News & World Report,* infilling is important because "the flip side of not dealing with our already developed areas is that we are dividing our society between rich and poor." The reason for infill, then, is to enhance the livability of the suburbs, as Gore likes to market the idea, by moving suburbanites into renovated urban areas. In a sense, "livability" is like forced busing for adults.

As Gore told the Brookings Institution in the big livability agenda speech he gave in 1998, "The mixed-use building of dwellings over small shops allowed people to work long hours, raise families close by, and start the climb up the economic ladder." He was hinting at the real agenda of New Urbanism, which, as movement gurus Richard Moe and Carter Wilkie explained in the *New Democrat,* calls "for a new pattern of development, inspired by the kind of neighborhoods and suburbs Americans built in the first two decades of the century, before traffic flow and isolated privacy overtook sidewalks and scenery as the goals."

The mixed-use city neighborhood was certainly "vibrant"— perhaps too much so, for it was this urban drama that families fled as soon as they could afford to, seeking more room, more privacy, more quiet and more security. Gore would force those families back to where they don't want to be and try to make them think they like it. Or, as *Forbes* magazine's Tim Ferguson put it, the New Urbanists' denser, smaller homes are "the housing equivalent of [a Ford] Escort."

Of course, there has to be a government bonus in the plan, something to make this denser housing and more crowded conditions seem like a bargain. So Gore has championed letting would-be homeowners qualify for larger federally-subsidized mortgages—which they'll need, because downtown housing sells at such a premium. His rationale for increasing the mortgage cap is that families will have more disposable income because they will save so much money by taking mass transit. In fact, Gore suggests giving new urban homebuyers "a 30-year transit pass." (Thus they can enjoy the double pleasure of a crowded bus by day and a more congested neighborhood by night.)

Many of the New Urbanist goals aren't necessarily bad. There is a role for more infill development, as my hometown of Oakland is demonstrating under the guiding hand of Mayor Jerry Brown. Public transit often does enhance communities. The problem is that New Urbanists don't quite understand human nature. Worse, to the extent that they understand it, they despise it. They are not filled with nostalgia for the teeming big city life of yesteryear so much as they are determined to force people into urban housing as a way of getting them out of their cars.

This is a much larger social engineering project than they may believe. Despite federal subsidies, despite national, state and local propaganda campaigns on behalf of public transit, and despite ever-worsening gridlock, only 5.1 percent of American commuters use public transit, according to a National Public Transportation survey. Yet the New Urbanists think that the only problem is a lack of toughness in their attacks on the car. In the Bay Area and Portland, for example, where rapid transit and light rail stations often lack sufficient parking, New Urbanists argue against increasing parking to increase ridership, insisting instead that commuters have an obligation to take buses to their rail stations.

Setting aside for the moment whether the New Urbanism is possible, the question remains: Is it desirable? Gore may romanticize village-like communities with great public transit that cuts commuting time and fattens the family budget, but statistics show that commuting on public transit in America takes on average about 80 percent longer than driving to work. According to the Nationwide Personal Transportation Survey of 1995, rail commuters' travel time to work was about fifty minutes, bus riders' commutes averaged over forty minutes, but drivers made it to work in slightly over twenty minutes. When you consider some of the New Urbanist–favored forms of public transit—such as snail-paced light rail, or better yet, taking the bus to get to snail-paced light rail—you see that their plans will do nothing to speed up the commute.

Gore also is relying on smoke and mirrors when he promises that his new communities will have cleaner air as a result of less congested traffic. While the air in America has been progressively cleaner each year since 1970, it is no surprise that air in high-density communities tends to be of poorer quality than the air in low-density communities.

Gore and his co-believers seem utterly oblivious to the central irony of this whole discussion: their prescription for cleaner air and less congestion would benefit only those homeowners who stayed in low-density suburbs, watching in satisfaction as a complete reversal of modern demographic trends inspired a massive exodus on the part of their neighbors to smaller, more expensive city homes. In other words, Gore's plan only reduces congestion for you if everyone else falls for the scheme, but you don't.

Government Sprawl

If he really is serious about preventing sprawl and overdevelopment, Al Gore should draw a ring—like the ones New Urbanists like to draw around urban areas—around the federal government and decree that its role will not grow beyond this boundary. The real sprawl in America may lie not in how far suburbs stretch from inner cities, but in how far the expanded role of government will stretch.

You can see the governmental sprawl in the Clinton administration's Web site www.livablecommunities.gov. The site hypes more than 150 programs funded by agencies you might have thought had nothing to do with the livability issue. You'd expect the Department of Housing and Urban Development, Department of the Interior, Department of Transportation and Environmental Protection Agency to be involved. But that's only the beginning. Livability partners also include a Department of Defense program concerning military base closures and another DOD program that provides access to hiking, biking and bird watching on military lands; a Department of Energy initiative that funds programs that promote "energy-efficient, environmentally friendly and affordable residences on a community scale"; a Department of Justice program that provides grants of $1.7 million to "promote the idea of community justice"; an Office of National Drug Control Policy program that funds intergovernmental substance-abuse reduction programs for youth; a Bureau of Alcohol, Tobacco and Firearms "gang-resistance education and training program"; a $180 million Department of Education program to make schools safer; an Office of the Comptroller of the Currency program to develop an academy of finance; a National Oceanic and Atmospheric Administration coastal management program; a U.S. Customs program designed to attract Boy Scouts to the Customs Service; a Department of Commerce program to help state and local governments develop and implement strategies for "changes in their economic situation"; a Department of Agriculture program to fund the building of "community facilities"; an Office of Thrift Supervisors program to promote community affairs programs; a Department of Treasury program that offers tax breaks to employers who hire ex-felons; a National Endowment for the Arts program to fund arts or humanities-based programs for "at-risk" kids; a Federal Emergency Management Agency (FEMA) program that pays for community disaster preparedness; an IRS program for first-time home buyers in the District of Columbia; a General Services Administration program that, among other feats, promotes government recycling of gas masks.

Livability, in other words, depends on growing the ganglia of government. Gore's agenda devotes some $1.3 billion to "securing safe streets" in the year 2000 alone, and proposes $600 million for "21st century community learning centers." It makes sense to assume that once these agencies and departments get a piece of the livability dollar, they will have a stake in keeping the program going, whether or not it works.

As chairman of Clinton's eighteen-member Community Enterprise Board, Al Gore has pushed to rework the enterprise zone strategy—providing tax incentives for employers to move into areas of urban blight—by adding government services. The administration worked out a plan that adds federal aid for health care, cops and construction to the mix, and in 1994 picked Atlanta, Chicago, Baltimore, New York City, Detroit and Philadelphia-Camden for $125 million each. Thus, "livability" is a stalking horse that carries federal money into troubled cities.

And this has been going on for years. Programs were entrenched before anyone knew enough about them to question the importance of, say, a federal program called "Let Kids Lead: Involving Youth in Transportation Choices," which had Missouri sixth- and seventh-graders working with local government officials on transportation planning decisions.

97

Roads Kill

Funding transit isn't good enough, not when people don't want to ride it, so Clinton/Gore has also given taxpayer money to environmental advocacy groups to try to scuttle road construction programs and generally scold drivers for not taking the bus.

In a five-year period, the EPA Transportation Partners program awarded $7.4 million in grants, without competitive bidding, to major environmental groups. Peter Samuel, the editor of the *Toll Road Newsletter,* started looking into the program in 1998. He discovered that the EPA grants included $1.4 million to the Environmental Defense Fund and another $1.4 million to the Surface Transportation Policy Project. Thus the administration essentially has been funding groups that sue to scuttle federal transportation projects, thereby creating costly delays and legal snarls.

"It has become almost a playbook maneuver," one aide to a GOP Senator told me. The Clinton/Gore administration hasn't wanted to take the heat for pushing too many environmental regulations, so it gives tax money to environmental groups that frequently sue the government and sometimes find a federal judge who will make an agency do what Clinton/Gore dare not order it to do.

Roy Kienitz, executive director of the Surface Transportation Policy Project, argues that his group is not anti-road. As proof, Kienitz has pointed out that he supported the federal transportation bill. Of course he did; it included more than $8 billion for non-road transportation projects. "Our organization is all about working to create more choices in the transportation system rather than fewer choices," he explained. But when the anti-car groups talk "choice," their real strategy is to oppose road-building in the expectation that traffic gridlock will become increasingly time-consuming and aggravating, thereby giving more and more commuters the idea that their only choice is to join car pools or take buses and light rail.

At one point, the Gore-oriented Transportation Partners Web site warned, "By relying on cars to get around, our roadways become congested, adding stress to our lives. Building bigger roads seems like the obvious answer, but it's an expensive short-term fix. Increasing capacity encourages driving, adds pollution to the air, creates congestion and puts pressure on officials to build even bigger roads at taxpayer expense. Adding lanes of traffic subtracts from our quality of life."

In a campaign to stop the building of roads to a new mall in Maryland, a group benefiting from a Transportation Partners grant warned that the roads "may put Marylanders' health at risk." It is wrong, the Environmental Defense Fund contended, to spend tax money "for new roads that bring sprawl and unhealthy air." The message is clear: Roads kill. As Peter Samuel observes, "Nowhere is there even a hint that use of motor vehicles provides people with benefits, [it is] as if everyone on the road is driving for frivolous and selfish reasons."

The enviros produce data to show that more roads result in more vehicle miles traveled. But they conveniently ignore the fact that cars emit less pollution when they're moving apace, as opposed to when they are stalled in gridlock while spewing gas fumes. By reducing time stuck in traffic, in other words, roads can actually work in behalf of air quality.

But the lieutenants in Gore's war against the car can't admit such a thing. On its Web site (which is partially funded by tax dollars), the Surface Transportation Policy Project lamented the "induced traffic" resulting from new roads. Executive director Roy Kienitz has argued, "Widening roads to ease congestion is ineffective and expensive at the same time. It's like trying to cure obesity by loosening your belt." Transportation writer Peter Samuel has a clever riposte: "While road critics...say that solving the transportation problem by adding new highway is like dealing with overweight by unbuckling your belt a few notches, limiting highways may be like refusing to buy new shoes for the kids because the better fitting shoes would only encourage their feet to grow."

Samuel observed that a favorite activity of EPA grantees is holding conferences. The National Pedestrian Conference. Cities for Climate Protection Campaign. Building Livable Communities. Rail-volution. Transportation Advocacy workshops in sixteen cities. He savors the image of all those committed public transportation advocates guzzling jet fuel and gasoline as they travel from city to city, to conferences where they discuss strategies to get other people to drive less.

Last year, EPA administrator and former Gore aide Carol Browner was forced to revamp the Transportation Partners program after Senator Robert Byrd, the freeway-loving ranking Democrat on the Senate Appropriations Committee, held hearings that questioned why the agency was funding anti-road activities. The EPA had claimed that Transportation Partners deserved credit for reducing vehicle miles traveled in the United States by 1.25 billion in 1997. But as economist Randal O'Toole noted, that was less than 0.1 percent of all driving that year. All those billions spent on public transit, all that lobbying for light rail lines and bicycle paths, and all that taxpayer-financed scolding of people in their cars—and the most that Al Gore and the other road-haters can point to is a statistically insignificant driving reduction that might have happened anyway without the program.

Call 211

If building roads is evil, it appears to be, for now, a necessary evil. But since the government has to have a solution for every problem, Gore needs to come up with some tax-funded non-asphalt solution for the unhappiness that is bound to happen on the highway. His answer is a national three-digit number, 211, that commuters could call from anywhere in the country to find out about traffic problems and public transit wherever they happen to be at any given moment. At Gore's urging, the Department of Transportation has petitioned the FCC for a license for the number.

"Information is one of the best weapons against traffic congestion," Gore told CNN when he announced the plan. "The more families know about their daily commute, or about road conditions during the day or on weekends, the better decisions they can make."

On the surface, making commutes easier may seem to contradict the vice president's campaign against the family car, but actually it is the other side of the same coin. Gore has figured out that because the road-hostile notions he has helped to promote mean that fewer roads are being built to accommodate the growing population, commuters will spend more frustrating hours going to and coming home from work each day. This means that Americans may spend about half a billion hours stuck in traffic each year, which gives them half a billion hours to think, stew and get angry. Since he is well known for pushing rails instead of roads, Gore doesn't want those stalled commuters to be angry with him. He wants at least to seem as though he is part of the solution, not a part of the problem.

And remember: He argues that his livability agenda reduces congestion and restores humanity. Or as he so smarmily put it, "A parent should not have to be saying good morning and good night to their child from a cell phone because they're stuck in traffic."

The 211 program would actually be an extension of various local traffic numbers already paid for with tax money. The reason for the federal three-digit number is that drivers would know what number to dial no matter where they were. I've tried the local number in the Bay Area, 817-1717. It was automated-voice-message hell. Press 1 for public transit, press 2 for information on freeway traffic, then press for the area where you live and enter the digits of the freeway you take. As I worked the buttons, I imagined all the cell phone users calling 211 and getting in ten-car pileups as a result, and never being able to say good night to their children at all.

Heaven on Earth

If there is a model for Goretopia, it is Portland, Oregon. Marveling at the city's decision to build a new light rail system, the vice president called Portland a city "with fewer arteries and more heart." In his Brookings livability speech, he said of Portland's Smart Growth plan, "They were told that it would be impossible—that the new emphasis on quality of life would force out businesses and force down property values. Instead, the opposite has come to pass: high-tech campuses spring up, home values have increased. Portland's population has swelled with families fleeing sprawl and congestion elsewhere—and a new light rail system has attracted 40 percent of all commuters in the city."

Gore is right about this much: In 1979 Portland created a regional planning authority called Metro. The goals of Metro's 2040 plan are promoting "livable neighborhoods," "protecting open space," reducing dependence on the automobile and accommodating "affordable housing." To prevent suburban sprawl, Metro, following the blueprint of the New Urbanists, drew a ring about the metropolitan area beyond which land should not be developed. As Metro critic Wendell Cox put it, "Portland seems to have chosen a future with two million cars in 500 square miles instead of 600 square miles."

But Gore is wrong about 40 percent of commuters using light rail. According to the Portland three-county transit authority (Tri-Met), 37 percent of people in the transit area used Tri-Met for at least *a round trip per month*. That's a far cry from 40 percent of all commuters riding Metro all the time. What's more, since Metro has forced developers to build in already developed areas and build more high-density housing, such as town houses and apartments, housing prices are up—good if you already own, but not such a great thing for young couples anxious to buy their first home. In 1989, Portland was an affordable city to buy a home in; by 1996 it had become one of America's five most expensive cities. In fact, housing was so expensive that Metro came out in favor of legislation to require builders to lower the prices of some 10 percent of their new homes. (And this, of course, would cause them to raise the prices for the remaining 90 percent).

Portland's latest light rail project, completed in 1998, cost just under a $1 billion. After building other projects connected to the light rail network, planners hope to reduce the percentage of auto trips made by car in the area from 92 percent to 88 percent. That might spell a welcome improvement if the population were not expected to increase by 75 percent, and traffic volume 50 percent, by 2015.

Jonathan E. D. Richmond, a fellow at Harvard's Kennedy School of Government, studied the light rail systems in fourteen cities and determined that Portland's regional transit planners wrongly got rid of a good bus service in order to accommodate more expensive light rail. Richmond concluded that only a third of the system's 27,000 average daily commuters were lured from their cars; the other two-thirds used to ride the bus. He denounced Portland transit planners' "obsession with technology"—which is rather choice when you consider how the New Urbanists are always putting down Americans' "obsession" with their cars.

G. B. Arrington, the regional transit system's planning director, admitted to the *Oregonian* that most current rail riders had once been bus riders. He disputed Jonathan Richmond's figures, but even if his own assertion that the rail line attracted 12,000 new riders in 1996 is correct, that's an awfully small gain for $1.2 billion.

The New Urbanists have a bizarre solution to the problem their ideology has helped to create: cut jobs. Area officials recently imposed a $1,000-per-job "growth impact fee" on Intel if it creates too many jobs. As Pacific Research Institute senior fellow Steven Hayward wrote in the *New York Times*, "Limiting jobs will certainly preserve the city's quality of life—for those who already have jobs. But are we so affluent and happy today that we can be indifferent to those without jobs or workers who aspire to move up? In Portland the answer, apparently, is yes."

Ironically, at the very moment Al Gore is directing the nation's attention to Portland, beleaguered Oregonians are turning away from his New Urbanist agenda. In 1996 voters rejected a referendum for a South-North light rail line by 53 percent to 47 percent. In 1998, they rejected a similar measure by a 52 percent to 48 percent margin. Now Portland transit chiefs are pushing for a scaled-back version of the line. Meanwhile, as Gore's heaven on earth was beginning to say no to light rail, it was also beginning to approve road projects. As Peter Samuel noted, "I think they're coming to their senses in Portland. They went to an extreme with a lot of these policies a few years ago and they're still living with some of that. They've done enough to see that it doesn't work."

▲

As Al Gore moves his presidential campaign into high gear, he spends more and more time telling people how they will live in Goretopia. But how does the vice president himself live? It's true he takes public transit, if you count taxpayer-funded Air Force Two as public transit. As for housing, from the time Gore was first elected to Congress until moving into the vice president's residence in the District of Columbia, Gore and family lived most of the year in a comfortable home in the suburbs of Virginia.

Gregg Easterbrook commented in *A Moment on the Earth,*

> *Gore has written of watching a glade of trees removed for a housing development near his Virginia home: "As the woods fell to make way for more concrete, more buildings, more parking lots, the wild things that lived there were forced to flee." Doesn't Gore live in a house? Park his car on concrete? Why are jets and homes and driveways only objectionable when somebody else desires them?*

CHAPTER FIVE

The Governess State

Early in the 2000 campaign, Al Gore stumped in favor of an Air-line Passenger Bill of Rights, a sort of airborne livability agenda which, among other things, would double the compensation for passengers bumped from oversold flights and require airlines to disclose when it books flights with puddle-jumper poor-cousin airlines. When he heard about the bill, Nebraska Democratic Senator Bob Kerrey, thinking of the important issues that faced the country, quipped sardonically, "All of a sudden, I'm going to pass a law saying, 'Give me sparkling water instead of plain water.' "

As Gore struggles to win the White House, he focuses more and more on sparkling water, and less on the truly thirsty. Under Clinton, the federal government's role was expanded into a "nanny state." In Goredom, the concept of hardship has expanded to cover not only surviving in the face of poverty and ignorance, but also dealing with delayed flights and having to monitor what CDs your children buy. In a Gore administration, the nanny state would become a strict governess, ever expanding her authority and nagging her citizens about proper behavior and correct thinking.

The government should not only provide public transportation, it should insist on people using it—for their own good. It should build more public transit, whether it is used or not. But if people don't use it, the government should scold them and then help them by providing a 211 traffic hotline.

Government under Gore would teach children values and relieve parents of some of the drudgery of parenting. He believes that it's the government's job to provide preschool and after-school programs for children—and not simply the children of single working moms, but also children with two married middle-class parents. And the government should relieve concerned parents of the obligation to get technology to block their children's access to bad Web sites. And it's the government's job to encourage people to engage in "life-long learning," hence a Gore-endorsed government tax credit available only to people who agree to be educated.

In Goretopia, every person is a mentor or has a mentor. A mentor, in fact, rather than a citizen, is the essential unit of the government. It is especially important that underclass children be mentored because it is inconceivable that they can succeed on their own.

The spiral of federal do-good programs Gore supports is already as dizzying as it is ineffective. There already are federal programs for reading, including federal programs to teach would-be teachers how to teach reading and programs to teach existing teachers how to teach reading and a program to teach college students how to teach reading. And if those programs don't work, then Gore's government will come up with other programs—like a program to push corporations to teach their workers how to volunteer as mentors to teach reading. If student reading achievement declines, this will only be taken as a sign that even more federal programs are needed.

The Clinton administration wants to pay for class-size

reduction in early grades, whether it improves learning or not. A Gore administration would pay for class-size reduction in *all* grades, whether it improves learning or not. Gore wants to require parents to sign contracts with their children's schools, promising to take on educational responsibilities, although the school people won't have to promise to do anything in return.

These measures are intended to create a sense of "community." Gore even imagines "community" as a college major. In the same vein, he envisions paid "volunteering" with a cushy benefits package to promote the spirit of volunteerism, and mandatory "volunteering" as a requirement for high-school graduation to ensure that volunteerism is a life-long commitment.

So that inner-city poor folk won't feel left out of the rush into the twenty-first century, Gore will give them computers and Internet access. And so that rural folks won't feel left out, the government will give them computers and Internet access, too. Then, if the new computer owners spend time online that they used to spend talking to their neighbors, thus experiencing cyber-alienation, there will be a federal program to boost community spirit.

In a Gore administration, every school will have Internet access. There will be free counseling at public schools for students who spend too much time on the Internet. There will be psychologists who can help students with their family problems, just like the staff counselors Gore brought into the White House. There will be anger management counseling for students who spend too much time playing violent video games on their computers instead of using the Internet to help with their homework.

And the best part of all: there will be no controlling legal authority.

▲

A sense of how far Gore's vision of government reaches can be gained from the brainstorm he had late one March evening in

1998. In an epiphany that shows the quirky techno-optimism that co-exists uneasily with his enviro-pessimism, Gore decided that the federal government should launch a satellite that would beam images of the earth over the Internet twenty-four hours a day. The satellite would be named Triana, after Rodrigo de Triana, the lookout who first spotted the New World from one of Columbus's ships. Triana would be educational and inspire young people to be interested in space. "It will help us reach new heights of understanding and insight," the vice president said.

It began with the sort of wool-gathering in which many politicians indulge, although few would try to turn it into a federal program. Or as House Majority Leader Dick Armey quipped, "This idea supposedly came from a dream. Well, I once dreamed I caught a ten-foot bass. But I didn't call up the Fish and Wildlife Service and ask them to spend $30 million to make it happen."

When Gore first proposed Triana, this flight of fancy was supposed to cost close to $20 million. Within seventeen months its budget rose to $50 million and then to $77 million—and that doesn't include the launch costs or education component which the vice president first cited as the raison d'être for the project. Finally, NASA's inspector general estimated that the ultimate price tag could run as high as $221 million.

The program's projected costs skyrocketed for two reasons. First, NASA originally underestimated costs and then wrongly expected that corporate largesse would fund part of the project. Also, boosters of the plan had left out the costs of labor, parts and the launch itself. And finally, the purpose of the project changed. Originally Gore touted Triana as an educational project that would inspire students to learn about space. Then—maybe because that idea seemed too, well, Gorish—NASA turned the mission into a research project that would collect global data.

Still, there wasn't much enthusiasm among space professionals. The inspector general noted, "We are concerned that

Triana's added science may not represent the best expenditure of NASA's limited science funding." Eileen Collins, the first woman to command an American space mission, said as much when she was asked about the project at the National Press Club. She replied, "There's some controversy as to where the money should be spent" in light of NASA's "very limited budget."

That "limited" budget is a sensitive issue. The Clinton budget for NASA in 1999 was described as so tight it could strangle the space program. As Representative Dave Weldon (R-Fla.) noted, "Indeed, there were actually six hundred people laid off because of a $100 million shortfall in the shuttle budget." Then when Gore, to whom Clinton had ceded control of NASA, came up with this idea, NASA miraculously found tens of millions of dollars.

NASA found the money, but it turned out that Gore's brainstorm was redundant. A number of Web sites, some also supported by tax dollars, already broadcast the earth as seen from a satellite, and it was therefore already possible to see all-earth, all-the-time. Clinton's point man for reinventing government and making it work more efficiently was eager to spend hundreds of millions of dollars for something Americans already can see for free at:

http://www.earthwatch.com

http://www.digitalearth.gov

http://motown.gsfc.nasa.gov/global.select/

http://globe.fsl.noaa.gov

These Web sites compelled the inspector general to suggest that instead of launching Triana, NASA should create a new project, "Triana: The Virtual Mission." As the inspector general said, "These images can be downloaded from government agencies, commercial companies (such as the Weather Channel and Earthwatch), and university and personal web sites." Best of all:

the budget for Virtual Triana would be a fraction of the cost of the real thing.

In 1999, the House Science Committee transferred $32 million from Triana toward cancer research. Later, House Republicans passed a measure making further funding for the project contingent on a study proving that Triana was a good use of taxpayer money. After the Science Committee vote, Gore spokesman Chris Lehane told reporters that the Republicans were "Luddites" who were bringing politics into science. But I think Representative James Sensenbrenner (R-Wis.) had it right when he dismissed Triana as a "multimillion-dollar screen saver."

The Tax Man Cometh

While I have discussed a number of areas—notably, abortion and the environment—in which his Disconnect has allowed Al Gore to make radical, unexplained shifts of position during his political career, there have been two causes to which he always has been faithful: higher taxes and increased federal spending. No other politician believes in government more than he does; no one wants to spread government into more nooks and crannies of our national life. As Al Gore sees it, the purpose of government is to grow.

The National Taxpayers Union named Gore the "Biggest Spender" in the Senate for three years from 1985 to 1992. "When he was a senator he had one of the biggest spending biggest taxing records of anyone in the chamber," the NTU's David Keating noted. "He holds a record that to this day has yet to be surpassed: To be named the Biggest Spender in the Senate for two consecutive years." Indeed, the organization ranked Gore a bigger spender than Massachusetts Senator Ted Kennedy in seven out of the eight years they were in the Senate together.

111

Gore voted for higher taxes or against lower taxes fifty-two times out of sixty-seven votes, or 78 percent of the time, from 1983 to 1994. And two of the fifteen taxpayer-friendly votes he made were in opposition to raising cigarette taxes—back in 1985, when Gore was still taking care of the interests of tobacco farmers back home.

When he ran for president in 1988, Gore said he didn't want to raise taxes, but if he had to—and with his love of new programs, he would have had to—he would not rule out a luxury tax, even though by 1988 the luxury tax already had devastated the boat-building industry in the United States and been exposed as a job killer. Gore also said he would consider raising the capital gains rate to 40 percent.

One doesn't hear much of this soak-the-rich rhetoric from Gore on the 2000 campaign trail. The NTU's David Keating speculates that the reason may be that the 1993 tax package's hikes on wealthy taxpayers were so steep—the top rate went to 39.6 percent, and the package took the lid off the salary cap for the 2.9 percent payroll tax for Medicare—that there isn't much room left for class warfare tax proposals. "It's hard to imagine" taxing affluent Americans more, Keating says. "No one really knows what the revenue maximization rate is, but they're probably not too far away from it."

In *Earth in the Balance*, Gore proposed revamping federal taxes by adding a hefty CO_2 tax to discourage energy consumption. Since the fateful demise of Clinton's BTU tax in 1993, he has shrunk away from such talk, despite the fact that energy taxes jibe with his global-warming agenda. Instead, despite a sizable projected surplus during the 2000 primary, Gore suggested a tax hike on tobacco as a way of funding another aspect of the moral uplift of his governess state.

▲

If the 211 cell-phone traffic line is one classic Gore proposal, the so-called "Gore Tax" on telecommunications to fund connecting every American classroom to the Internet is another. The Gore Tax is a classic because it is so invisible that most people don't realize they are paying it. (What they don't know won't hurt them, or him.) The National Taxpayers Union has reported that phone companies are charging their customers between 5 and 5.9 percent to pay this new levy—on top of a 3 percent excise tax already tacked onto long distance telephone calls.

Gore says he is proud that pundits named the tax, also known as the e-rate, after him. It may be regressive in its fiscal implications, but it is a progressive tax, he believes, in its social benefits. And it is very kind to politicians in that the tax is invisible not only to the people who pay it, but also to Congress, which doesn't have to vote on it, and to the president, who doesn't have to sign any bill. The $2.4 billion tax was levied by the Federal Communications Commission in relative obscurity.

Aside from its origins as a stealth maneuver, however, the tax is also quintessentially Gore because the money is spent on technology, an area dear to Gore's image of himself as the first twenty-first-century politician. There's no pretense of local control. Schools cannot use the tax to buy books or desks or fund teachers' aides, even if administrators believe such things would help their students most; the tax only subsidizes spending for high tech. One member of the FCC, Commissioner Harold Furchtgott-Roth, who voted against the Gore Tax, dismissed the program as corporate welfare, with the beneficiaries being "hardware and software providers"—many of whom, I would add, are Gore contributors.

Since President Clinton ceded the area of high tech to Gore, the e-rate always has been a Gore production, and has thus involved Gore patronage. A Gore crony and fundraiser, Ira Fishman, headed the program that distributed e-rate funds to public schools. It began as the Schools and Libraries Corporation, but later was folded into the Universal Service Administrative Corporation after the General Accounting Office questioned the legality of the SLC. Fishman was paid an annual salary plus bonus of $250,000—a figure so outrageous that it created a furor that ended only with Fishman's resignation in 1998 and his replacement by a successor who took a 40 percent pay cut.

Just as the Gore Disconnect has allowed the vice president to claim innocently that he never profited from tobacco or supported abortion, so it enables him to claim that he is a tax cutter rather than a big spender. In a July 1999 speech he said, "I have long supported tax cuts for the middle class. Since the day I proposed a broad middle-class tax cut as a member of the Senate, I have been fighting for the right kind of tax relief."

In fact, Gore's tax cut plan—trimming $250 to $300 million over ten years when the surplus will rise to an estimated $3 trillion—is so modest that he forgot to include it as a separate item in a ten-year budget plan posted on his Web page.

As a candidate in 2000, Gore presented a tax cut plan that would reduce the marriage penalty by increasing the standard deduction and allow poor families to earn more and still qualify for the Earned Income Tax Credit. Gore says he supports President Clinton's USA Accounts, which would give money to poor workers for savings, but didn't include funding for the proposed new program in the budget he used to justify his campaign promises. Plan Gore also includes 401(j) accounts that allow taxpayers to put aside a tax-free $2,500 annually for education, with a small credit if they earn under $40,000. But to call that package a "middle class tax cut" is like calling an hors d'oeuvre a six-course meal.

Worst of all, the rest of Gore's tax reduction package goes not to working families, but to high-tech companies and other corporations that would benefit from his proposal to make research and development tax credits permanent. An incredulous Ralph Nader refers to this giveaway as a "tip" from Gore to big-donor industries: "Now why in the world, with one of the most lucrative industries in the world, one of the most heavily tax-subsidized industries, do you have to bribe them to do research and development for new products, which is what they're all about? With taxpayer money? We're dealing with a credit, that's a lot better than a deduction. That's like a cash transfer from the U.S. treasury."

Gore spent the presidential primary season posing as the one trustworthy defender of the non–Social Security federal surplus, about $1 trillion of surplus funds above those dedicated to Social Security. In the fall of 1999, Gore chastised Bill Bradley for not presenting a solid financial accounting of his proposed health plan and for spending the surplus on one program. He called Bradley's proposals "promises without price tags."

Of course, Gore himself hadn't made public any numbers for his own proposals. His aides would say that the cost of, say, his universal preschool plan would be released when Gore later released his budget plan. When Bradley partisans called him on this, Gore revealed that he did go over the numbers—which he still had not shared with the public—with a few select journalists. Later on, Team Gore claimed to have posted his budget on the Internet. But all they had done was slap on a pie chart, devoid of details and not giving any information as to how much universal preschool and other programs might actually cost. When journalists were finally able to check Gore's estimates, they found that his campaign had low-balled shamelessly. For example, he set aside $50 billion for universal preschool over ten years, when it could cost as much as $200 billion. (Gore leaves one fact out of his speeches for fear of revealing that his preschool giveaway isn't such a bargain: states would have to pick up half the freight.) When the media called Gore on this, he modified his proposal to cover fewer children, although true to form, he would continue to tell audiences that his proposal was universal.

When Bill Bradley admitted that he was willing to raise taxes to fund his health plan if economic forces required it, he gave Gore a club with which he ruthlessly beat him. "To propose a possible tax increase, not because of some contingency related to unknowns in the economy but because of an inability to cover a huge gaping hole in a campaign promise that can't be covered in any other way—that is irresponsible," the vice president clucked.

Yet while Gore postured as the fiscally responsible one, analysts concluded that both he and Bradley had proposed spending that would have to eat into the surplus. Gore's own health care expert estimated that his health plan would cost $312 billion over ten years—or more than double the $146 billion Gore allotted for it. Another adviser conceded to the *Baltimore Sun* that Gore had tapped out the surplus. As the National Taxpayers Union head David Keating says of Gore, "I wouldn't trust Al Gore not to raise taxes at all. I don't think he can be trusted on the issue. If you add up his spending promises, you count on his unwillingness to reform entitlement programs, either he's going to raise taxes a lot in a Gore administration or we start running big deficits. Or the next administration would be left with a huge fiscal problem."

The Man Who Reinvented Government

When President Clinton was divvying up responsibilities early in his administration, Al Gore wanted welfare reform, but didn't get it. His consolation prize was Reinventing Government, aka

REGO. The vice president likes to joke that REGO is Gore spelled sideways, but what was really funny was that he should get this job at all given the fact that he had earned a 1989–1992 rating of 11.1 percent from Citizens Against Government Waste. Nonetheless, Gore took on the reinventing government job with a passion, and reinvented it in his own image.

In a 1999 interview with the magazine *The Business of Government,* the vice president made two claims about his Reinventing Government effort. He said, "We've created a government that works better and costs less." And he said the administration had made government "the smallest since the administration of President Kennedy" and reduced the federal workforce by more than 350,000 full-time employees. Gore was right to take credit for making some branches of the government run better, but his claim that government has grown smaller under Clinton/Gore is a joke.

REGO efforts did manage to pare down the number of middle managers in the federal workplace by some 35,000. That was no small feat. As the Brookings Institution's Paul Light noted in his book *The True Size of Government,* Presidents Nixon, Ford and Reagan launched similar efforts to reduce the number of middle managers and failed. Gore also used REGO to eliminate niggling regulations and streamline the purchasing process. Lampooning a federal guideline that called for smashing an ashtray with a hammer to see if the make was defective, Gore went on David Letterman and made a show of smashing an ashtray with a hammer. He had a great photo op with Clinton and two forklifts stacked with government regulations he had targeted for destruction.

But does the government, as Gore claims, work better and cost less? According to Paul Light, "the shadow of government"— that is, federal workers, grant recipients, military troops, postal employees and contract workers—hit nearly seventeen million people, "a number nine times larger than the one people used to declare the era of big government over." The federal budget was barely over $1.409 trillion in 1993 when Clinton came to office and exceeds $1.8 trillion in the year 2000.

One could argue that REGO is largely the peace dividend, since military cuts account for about three-quarters of the job reductions. An additional 14,500 positions came from the Federal Deposit Insurance Corporation, which naturally was downsized after the cleanup of the savings-and-loan debacle.

That is not to say that REGO did not eliminate other positions. As Light notes, non-defense civilian employment fell by nearly 100,000 jobs between 1993 and 1996. But while the federal government decreased the number of federal workers, it increased the number of grant recipients and contract workers. Under Clinton/Gore the federal government expanded into areas traditionally administered by state and local governments. The administration put 100,000 local police on the federal payroll. Then it started to hire 100,000 teachers for local school districts.

Meanwhile, for all of Gore's trimming activities, the payroll for major agencies rose from $5.9 billion to $7.4 billion. After Gore ostensibly pared down government to such a point that the administration was arguing that it could not abide by very modest cuts—less than 1 percent—proposed by the GOP in 1999, there were still 186,000 contract employees in the Department of Agriculture alone, according to Representative Tom Coburn (R-Okla.).

Paul Light argues that it is impossible to know how big the government workforce is—largely because the administration never really wanted to know. Democratic Senator David Pryor wrote to members of the administration, including Gore, asking them to work on an accurate count of the real "federal workforce," including contracted employees, and received a response from the Office of Management and Budget refusing that request on the grounds that "It is not all clear...that the benefits of such an effort would exceed its costs."

Of course, if REGO had been as tough a process as Gore liked to paint it, he probably wouldn't have garnered all those public employee union endorsements, and chances are that the National Treasury Employees Union president would not have gushed to the *Washington Post* about how Gore "has really been a leader on issues that affect federal employees." And the Center of Responsive Politics would not have reported in June 1999 that Gore campaigns had received some $247,427 from bureaucrats and public officials.

▲

By 1995, Gore had named the $77 million "Citizenship USA" project, with a mandate to reduce the backlog of citizenship applications, as one of the major components of REGO. (Immigration and Naturalization Service chief Doris Meissner would boast that the program would put the "N" back in INS.) Citizenship USA targeted five big cities where 75 percent of applications are filed— Chicago, L.A., Miami, New York and San Francisco—for expedited citizenship processing.

In the background of this project was a meeting that occurred the previous September when Daniel Solis, then director of the United Neighborhood Organization, had the good luck to find himself seated next to President Clinton at a Democratic Party event at Chicago's Eli's Steakhouse. Solis used the opportunity to pitch Clinton with an idea: encouraging immigrants to become fast-track citizens so that they could register as Democrats. According to Solis, this could be a more effective way to attract votes than getting existing citizens to register and vote. Clinton liked what he heard and put Solis in touch with aides Harold Ickes and Rahm Emanuel.

Using REGO to invent new Democrats became a Gore operation. Gore aides tried to figure out how to maximize what an aide admitted could be seen as "a pro-Democratic voter mill." A draft staff memo suggested that the administration "lower the standards for citizenship" by lowering the interpretation of basic knowledge of civic and good moral character.

One Gore aide, Doug Farbrother, went so far as to suggest that INS deputy commissioner Chris Sales be moved to another job and that he, Farbrother, be made deputy commissioner in his place. In March 1996, Farbrother e-mailed Gore with a complaint that "unless we blast INS headquarters loose from their grip on the frontline managers, we are going to have way too many people still waiting for citizenship in November." Farbrother also e-mailed Gore that the INS was not doing enough to "produce a million new citizens before election day." Among his other suggestions, Farbrother wanted to hire temps to process applications, to "waive stupid rules, move money from one account to another as needed and recruit and hire people locally," and to "waive extensive background investigations on new employees."

Deputy Attorney General Jamie Gorelick wrote to INS Commissioner Doris Meissner delegating full authority "to waive, suspend or deviate from non-statutory policies, regulations and procedures to enhance the speed and convenience of the process for those who do." The White House told the INS to extend hours to process more applications, and ten days later the INS began working weekends.

The administration's determination to expedite citizenship in time for the 1996 general election turned into a chaotic free-for-all. Gore once told a Hispanic group that his people were working on a "reinvention lab to expedite the FBI's fingerprint checks." That reinvention, reported the syndicated columnist Tony Snow, may have been a "dumpster that served as the final resting place for between 4,000 and 6,000 troublesome files from Los Angeles alone." The *Chicago Tribune* reported that at one massive swearing-in of new citizens, the INS didn't even collect green cards, which were going for $30,000 on the street. Worst of all, the INS allowed 180,000 people, including 30,000 in New York City alone, to become citizens without criminal background checks. A new policy directed the INS to proceed with processing citizenship applications if the FBI background check division didn't advise against it within sixty days, although, as the *Washington Times* later reported, some INS officials were well aware that it took the FBI 70 to 166 days to screen applicants with criminal histories. While the administration had done a fine job pushing the INS to process applications faster, apparently no one ever told FBI Director Louis Freeh about the need to gear up for a record number of background checks or about the new sixty-day policy.

Within a month of the 1996 election, and after weeks of stories about flaws in the program, the administration announced an end to the Citizenship USA practice of processing citizenship papers if the INS had not heard otherwise from the FBI fingerprint division within sixty days. Said an INS spokesman, "The election had absolutely nothing to do with the timing of the policy change."

The INS later determined that 71,557 people with arrest records became U.S. citizens during this frenzied push, a group that included 16,400 adults who had been arrested for felonies. A congressional review of some 20,000 files found more than 29,000 criminal charges, including murder, rape and sexual assault. About a third of those applicants had convictions, more than 1,000 of them for crimes that would automatically disqualify a request for citizenship.

The irony is that if one of these new citizens commits a heinous crime, and an enterprising journalist connects the dots,

Al Gore could have a Willie Horton of his own waiting in his future—especially since INS attempts to deport a small number of these new citizens have been stalled in the courts. As K. C. McAlpin of the immigration watchdog group Federation for American Immigration Reform noted, "It could still be years before this issue is resolved."

But the number of new citizen/criminals was less important to Team Gore than the 1.3 million "Instant Democrats"—as the *National Review* called them—who were sworn in so that they could vote in 1996.

Corporate Welfare

The big legislative success of the Clinton administration was welfare reform, an effort which the president had delayed working on, despite his campaign rhetoric, until congressional Republicans finally forced him to approve a bill. Clinton had vetoed earlier welfare reform bills, but Gore reportedly pushed President Clinton to sign the bill in 1996 when other aides wanted him to veto it. Credit the administration with not stopping the reform train. The number of families on welfare decreased from 4.73 million in 1995 to 2.98 million in 1998.

Yet while the number of poor families on welfare has fallen dramatically, the administration has failed to trim the caseload of affluent companies on corporate welfare. It's not as if these big corporations are needy. As the Cato Institute's Steve Moore testified before Congress in 1999, "In 1997, the Fortune 500 corporations recorded best-ever earnings of $325 billion, yet incredibly Uncle Sam doled out nearly $75 billion in taxpayers subsidies." When he crunched those numbers, Moore estimated that corporate welfare has increased to the tune of almost 10 percent over the last four years.

As Ralph Nader testified before the House Budget Committee in 1999, the administration did little or nothing about halting the giveaway of national resources to large corporations, some of which are not even American companies. Nader figured that charging companies that mine in national parks an 8 percent royalty could net some $200 million annually. Yet Gore, the administration's point man on the environment, only moved to charge these fees when he needed money to fund his anti-sprawl initiatives.

But he is kindest of all to agribusiness. While Candidate Gore argued that the GOP proposal for a 10 percent across-the-board individual tax cut was essentially immoral, he was traipsing through electorally significant farm states calling for a boost in farm subsidies and other forms of welfare for agribusiness. "Here we have the biggest surpluses in the history of the world," Gore said in one speech, "and that bunch in control in there is trying to blow it all on a risky tax scheme while the whole farm sector of our economy is on the verge of absolute bankruptcy."

In 1999, Washington budgeted $8.7 billion in emergency aid for American farmers—aid that essentially was funded by a bipartisan raiding of the surplus, which Gore claimed to be committed to defending to his last breath. In his familiar apocalyptic mode, Gore said the money was needed to mitigate "the worst crisis our farmers have ever experienced." From 1993 to 1998, the number of American farms did indeed decline by 10,000—which might sound like a crisis if you didn't know there are 1.9 million farms in America. As the *New York Times* reported, Gore's "worst crisis" entailed a drop in farm revenue from $44.1 billion in 1998 to $43.8 billion in 1999—less than one percent. This crisis generally had nothing to do with the weather, and everything to do with the fact that many farmers had over-planted and were reaping bountiful harvests, which lead to low prices. Of course, the crisis was all that more dire because it affected the important primary states of Iowa and New Hampshire. So Gore wanted American taxpayers to pony up an additional $8.7 billion for farmers, after a $6 billion "emergency" bail-out the year before and on top of the $12 billion they receive annually.

As Cato's Steve Moore testified, over 80 percent of farm subsidies go to farmers with a net worth of more than $500,000.

In the first presidential debate of the new millennium, Gore planted an Iowa farmer in the Iowa audience, then asked him to stand up so Bill Bradley could explain to him why he voted against a 1993 flood-relief bill that had bailed the farmer out after his crops were destroyed. Bradley was dumbfounded. He had voted *for* the major disaster relief package, and it had passed the Senate unanimously. It was true that Bradley had opposed an amendment by Iowa Senator Tom Harkin for even more disaster relief because he did not believe it was targeted to those who needed aid the most. As a Bradley campaign piece later explained, the administration also had opposed that measure until minutes before the floor debate ended.

Presidential Politics

In September 1999, as his presidential campaign was getting into gear, Gore released a reasonable plan for expanding access to health care. He wanted to expand eligibility for the under-utilized Children's Health Insurance Program to children in families with incomes of up to 250 percent of the poverty level, or about $41,750 for a family of four. Gore also proposed a 25 percent tax credit for individuals who buy their own health insurance and his plan allowed the seven million parents of uninsured children to buy coverage for themselves as well. Gore underestimated the plan's cost by more than half, and he failed to suggest any cuts in corporate welfare to fund the new program, but he knew enough not to repeat the Hillary health plan fiasco. "We have learned that we cannot overhaul the system in one fell swoop," he announced. "Experience has taught us that there is a way to keep what is right, while fixing what is wrong with American health care."

It is doubtful that the vice president would have been so incremental in his approach if Bill Bradley had gone first with his health proposal. After all, Gore's modus operandi throughout the primary had been to promise more than the other guy. But Gore went first in this case and so Bradley was able to outbid him by coming up with a more generous plan providing tax credits that would subsidize premiums for low-income families both with and without insurance. Then, Bradley attacked Gore for not caring enough about the poor, because Gore had not proposed universal coverage, as he had done.

Gore charged, probably correctly, that Bradley's solution likely would cost taxpayers more than $1 trillion over ten years, as opposed to the $650 billion Bradley said it would cost. But then the vice president got nasty, attacking Bradley for voting in the Senate to consider raising the retirement age to seventy, even though Gore had also been on the panel that considered it. He hit Bradley for proposing to eliminate Medicaid (and replace it with private coverage), even though he himself had chaired hearings that explored doing the same thing. Then, to hone his assault, he told minority audiences that the Bradley plan would adversely affect poor blacks and Latinos, and warned the gay community that it would shortchange people with AIDS.

During the primary's many debates, Gore repeatedly referred to Bradley's plan as one that would award "vouchers" that were "capped" at $150 per month. Bradley repeatedly responded that he had not proposed vouchers, but tax credits, and that the $150 was not a cap, but a proposed average subsidy per individual.

Gore kept repeating these misrepresentations until he had gotten completely under Bradley's skin. It was clear from the look of disgust on Bradley's face during their debates that he was so angry he couldn't think straight or talk tough. You could see him thinking, with a combination of disgust and envy, "How does this guy get away with this?"

▲

In October 1999, the man who prided himself on being an activist vice president told *Los Angeles Times* reporter Edwin Chen that as a result of his campaign for the presidency he had now decided to spend less time on his official duties. "It's a breaking away process," Gore explained.

Asked if the new approach might hurt him, Gore responded, "I hope not. But if it does, then so be it. I hope not. But that's not particularly important compared to making sure my line of communication with the American people is strong and clear." And: "I've finally figured out to let go of the vice presidential trappings...and to let go of some of the campaign approaches that seemed right for a vice president campaigning on behalf of a president's policies—but really didn't suit me campaigning for myself." As this conversation took place, Gore and Chen were seated in one of those trappings, Air Force Two, and about to land at another, Andrews Air Force Base.

Yet while Gore was allegedly liberating himself from the confines of the vice presidency, he was treating himself to more perks than ever. Within weeks, he would meet with cabinet members to find programs and awards he could announce, which would allow him to campaign for office while traveling to events, naturally in key electoral states, on the public dime. He had spent so much of his campaign money already—and the total Gore could spend was capped by a federal law he supported—that he would need every dollar of taxpayer backing he could get to make it through to the Democratic convention.

President Clinton played along with Gore's effort to mine government for free publicity in which he could play Santa Claus. In 2000, with the help of Gore supporters in Silicon Valley, Clinton and Gore launched a billion-dollar government program called ClickStart to hook up poor families to the Internet. Clinton mentioned the program during his State of the Union speech. Gore pronounced computer literacy "a fundamental civil right."

A fundamental civil right? Already high tech had become so cheap that one company was offering Internet access and a personal computer for $300 per year, and other companies were offering free access for those who already had computers. Yet Gore advocated the program as he sought to curry favor with racial and ethnic minorities. He promised to close "digital divide" even when Massachusetts-based Forrester Research had discovered that Latinos, blacks and Asians had begun to sign up for the Internet faster than whites, which meant the divide was already closing. In other words, the market was taking care of the problem. Wade Rendlett, a corporate booster of the ClickStart program and Gore adviser, admitted that within five years Internet access would be so cheap—even less than $300 per year—that there would be no need for the government to help the poor get online. When that time came, Rendlett said, he trusted Congress to kill Gore's program.

Of course, if he is wrong, and this is just another attempt to turn Silicon Valley into America's next welfare queen, taxpayers foot the bill as a rich industry gets even richer.

CHAPTER SIX

Gore in EduLand

"**A**ll the research and all the experiences of parents have shown very clearly that most learning takes place in the first few years of life and if kids get off to a great start before they ever get to kindergarten, the chances for them to succeed in life, to have good jobs, to lead fulfilling lives, are greatly enhanced," said Al Gore of his plan to offer universal preschool, centerpiece of his promise to "revolutionize education."

Actually, this preschool revolution has been going on since Head Start was launched in 1965 as part of President Lyndon Johnson's War on Poverty. Over thirty-four years, the federal government has spent some $35 billion on the program. With its promise of raising achievement scores and social skills among poor students, the program has always been popular, even if its actual results have been ambiguous. "The idea was that if you give poor children a head start, then they'll catch up to middle-class kids," explained Kay Hymowitz, author of *Ready or Not: Why Treating Children as Small Adults Endangers Their Futures and Ours*. "It hasn't worked out that way. Instead you find second- and third-generation Head Starters—but some people don't seem to have noticed."

In 1997 the General Accounting Office concluded that "the body of research on current Head Start is insufficient to draw conclusions about the impact of the national program." Analyst Darcy Olsen noted in a paper for the libertarian Cato Institute that most studies of preschool "have significant methodological problems. They are impaired by small sample size, attrition, and selection bias. Furthermore, most programs studied are model programs, not large scale programs, which means they are severely limited in statistical power and generalizability."

One of the two studies most frequently cited in support of preschool for the disadvantaged is "Significant Benefits: The High/Scope Perry Preschool Study Through Age 27," written by High/Scope Research Director Lawrence J. Schweinhart, and focusing on three- and four-year olds deemed "at risk." The report concluded that preschool graduates had completed an average of 11.9 years of school, versus 11 years completed by the control groups. Participants were less likely to be arrested for drug dealing. Some 59 percent of the program's graduates went on welfare as adults, as opposed to 80 percent of nonparticipants. Schweinhart also found that participants were more likely than nonparticipants to earn more than $2,000 per month and more likely to be employed at the time of their interview. Participants also were more likely to own homes—36 percent versus 13 percent—and second cars.

Schweinhart added up the costs to taxpayers that would have been incurred if the participants' prison time, welfare benefits, special education costs and other government-funded expenses matched those of the control group, and concluded that the High/Scope program saved the taxpayers "a return on investment of $7.16 on the dollar." (The program cost was $7,252 per child per year in 1992 dollars, by his reckoning.) This $7 figure is frequently cited in pro-preschool literature. California's Universal Preschool Task Force, for instance, repeated the line that the program "yielded more than $7 in benefits for every $1 invested" in its report suggesting universal preschool for three- and four-year olds. It did not point out peculiarities in the Schweinhart study (a parent of participating children had to be home during the day, for instance, while the parents of control group children did not) that might have called its conclusions into question. On the basis of the experience of fifty-eight students in one study, therefore, funding of the program has reached nearly $5 billion per year and the program has been expanded to care for 860,000 children,

The other study that boosters cite involved the Abecedarian Project in Chapel Hill, North Carolina, which started in 1972. The study did find that at age fifteen, preschool graduates scored an average of 4.6 points higher on IQ tests than children in the control group. But the Abecedarian project started working with children at a median age of 4.4 months. The program provided year-round services for eight hours per day for five days a week. (Most preschool programs involve a half-day session during the school year for older children.) Participants received free medical care and social services. What's more, as Darcy Olsen noted, "the Abecedarian Project has not been replicated."

In June 1999, the *San Francisco Chronicle* ran a wire service story on the "Cost, Quality and Child Outcomes" study, which reported, "The United States' longest-running effort to gauge the effects of day care centers on children has found that for all children—but particularly for those most at risk of academic failure—good day care boosts school performance in second grade." But the study didn't test children in good preschool programs versus children outside of preschool; it compared children in what it considered to be good day care programs with children attending what researchers figured were bad programs. Moreover, the study buried its more important finding, that most child care in America is "well below what the early childhood profession recognizes as high quality." So if most preschool is mediocre, why expand it? Wouldn't it make more sense to improve existing preschool than to expand what boosters themselves often refer to as a sub-par program? But fixing what's broken would keep Gore from offering a new babysitting benefit to overtaxed middle-class parents whose income precludes them from signing up with federal programs for the disadvantaged.

Of course, most middle-class parents wouldn't want to send their children to poor or mediocre preschool programs, such as those that comprise nearly three-quarters of California preschools, according to a state task force study. Thus Gore—who raked primary opponent Bill Bradley over the coals for having voted for an experimental educational voucher program for failing public schools—endorses vouchers for preschool. Consider it Gore's way of buying off opposition from the burgeoning private preschool and day care industry. It is a position that wouldn't wash anywhere except in EduLand: no to vouchers for poor and primarily minority families whose children are consigned to violent, substandard schools that spawn illiteracy; yes to vouchers for middle-class families that wouldn't tolerate these conditions for an instant for their preschool children.

Gore has adopted the latest trendy "science" which claims, as he put it, that "all research and all experience of parents have shown very clearly that most learning takes place in the first few years of life." He bases this hyperbole on research that shows rapid brain development among young laboratory animals (largely rodents), especially when they are introduced to the proper stimuli. If his assertion were true—and it's most probably not—many children would be better off at home where the stimulation would involve loving attention. If his assertion were true, that would provide an extra reason why Gore should be advocating tax breaks that allow one parent to stay home in a child's first years—which would be good for children regardless of the timing of brain development.

To keep his universal preschool plan from being a budget breaker, Gore capped the cost of federal funding at $2,700 per child—which suggests that these programs, whatever their intrinsic value, would be limited in how much instruction they could include. At times Gore has promised to make the universal preschool program available to all three- and four-year-olds. But when pressed by those who point out that he hasn't set aside enough funding for all those children, he has retreated to promising preschool for all four-year-olds, with services for three-year-olds when the money is available. Then, when away from the fiscal types, he has gone back to promising universal access to preschool for all three- and four-year-olds.

The Politics of Class Size

Another central plank in Gore's education platform is reduced class size. As in the case of his preschool proposals, he calls his idea "revolutionary," although class-size reduction has long since been applied in California, Indiana, Tennessee and Texas. It has also been endorsed by the federal government in the sense that the administration's program to hire 100,000 teachers is part of its national class-size reduction initiative. The program actually has only hired 30,000 teachers. Nonetheless, Gore wants the program to be bigger, more dramatic, so he has proposed reducing class size in grades K–12 instead of early grades only, and promised to go a little further than most states by reducing class size to eighteen students per teacher (as opposed to twenty, which is the rule in California and elsewhere) in early grades and twenty students in later grades.

As in the case of universal preschool, Gore has shown himself to be so intent on offering a payout to the educational establishment that he has ignored research suggesting that his "revolutionary" reform probably won't bring the sort of improvements parents should expect from a program with such huge costs.

The experience of California—a leader in the attempt to grapple with class size and the object of Gore's constant attention because of its mother lode of electoral votes—should have been educational for him. The Class Size Reduction Research Consortium, which was mandated by the California legislature to study effects of the class-size reduction program instituted by Governor Pete Wilson in 1996, found very modest gains for such a big-ticket item. After expenditures of more than $1 billion extra per year, the percentage of third-graders who scored above the 50th national percentile in math and language rose only by 2 to 4 percent.

This may be because California's grand experiment sharply increased the demand for teachers, which forced districts to hire an unusually high number of teachers with less than three years' experience. Districts with poor students tended to hire less experienced teachers. As Oakland school board member Jean Quan told the *San Francisco Chronicle*, "In some cases, it may have been wiser to keep a teacher with that extra 10 kids than to flop them into a classroom without a trained teacher."

The U.S. Department of Education reviewed studies on class-size reduction. It found a 1986 review concluding that class-size reductions in the early grades, particularly kindergarten through grade three, could have positive effects, although improvement was less likely to occur if a change in teaching methods did not accompany decreased class size. Another study found gains when the student/teacher ratio dropped to 18/1 in grades one through seven. A 1997 analysis by the National Center for Education Statistics found higher math achievement in the fourth and eighth grade. Tennessee reported increased test scores—moving the state from the bottom to near the middle in second-grade test scores—due to its K–3 class-size reduction.

But other studies reported little or no gain from smaller classes. One researcher who studied data from the 1950s to 1986 concluded that the research "did not justify a policy to reduce class size in view of the costs involved and the potential negative impact on the quality of the teaching force." A study of Florida classrooms found no relationship between smaller classes and student achievement. Another analysis found class-size reduction to be too expensive for what it achieved and posited that less expensive measures could result in even higher achievement.

High-achieving parochial schools have larger class sizes than public schools. Countries whose schools routinely have classes of forty students or more have scored higher on international tests than the United States. As Hoover Institution Senior Fellow Edward P. Lazear wrote in the *Los Angeles Times*, "Blanket policies of class-size reduction are inefficient and wasteful. A targeted approach would be best. Schools that have disadvantaged or many special-needs children might want class-size reductions, whereas other schools might be better off allocating their funds in other ways."

In March 1999 the Department of Education released a study that found there was a consensus that class-size reduction leads to higher student achievement in early grades, but noted that researchers "are more cautious about the question of positive effects of class-size reduction in the 4th through 12th grades." Why then would Gore want to reduce class size to twenty students in later grades? And for that matter, why push for a national reduction in early grades when California's experiment produced so little for so much? Why not call for targeted class-size reductions if research finds certain students and schools most likely to benefit? The answer is clear: Gore knows that class-size reduction is popular with middle-class voters—so it doesn't matter if it works or not.

Gore suggests a 21st Century Teacher Corps that would reward college students with $10,000 if they choose to teach in schools with disadvantaged children. Gore also wants to award bonuses of $10,000 to adults willing to switch to teaching careers. Why pay people to become teachers? Having pushed for class-size reductions that will drive up the demand for teachers, Gore predicts a teacher shortage.

The politics of class size allows Gore to trump the Clinton administration's budgeted $12.4 billion to hire 100,000 new teachers as a way of rewarding the teachers' unions, which, according to the Center for Public Integrity, gave the Democratic National Committee $4.6 million from 1991 to June 1999. Universal preschool and class-size reduction guarantee the unions an appreciable swelling of their ranks. More members mean more dues and more dues mean more contributions.

It is the political equivalent of perpetual motion.

▲

Knowing that he is viewed as the teachers' unions' kept candidate, Gore tries to demonstrate his independence by going after incompetent teachers. "No teaching license should be a lifetime job guarantee," he has said. He has called for more teacher testing, tougher standards for teachers, bonuses for master teachers and teachers who received national certification, and evaluations to certify teachers every five years. All this sounds like a get-tough policy, but it is a script approved by the National Education Association and American Federation of Teachers as a way of protecting the status quo from attacks—and the threat of real change—by educational reformers.

It's not as if teachers' unions, supporters of Gore's allegedly tough measures, have a good record when it comes to standards and teacher testing. When California developed a test for minimal competence, its California Basic Education Skills Test (CBEST), testing for tenth-grade mastery in math, reading and writing, lawsuits made the state dumb down the math to the eighth-grade level. The California Teachers Association wrote an amicus brief in support of a lawsuit, charging that the test was racist. The California Federation of Teachers boldly remained neutral.

As for his support of testing teachers every five years and removing bad teachers who fail to improve with mentoring, Gore knows, and the unions do too, that the federal government can't impose those requirements on local school districts with collective bargaining agreements. He can promise big on this, and the teachers' unions can stand shoulder to shoulder with him, without ever having to worry about these notions being put to the test.

The Politics of Parental Involvement

Gore said it in his May 1999 education speech and it has become a truism in EduLand: "We need more parental involvement in our schools." The previous January, he had announced that the administration was proposing a $10 million increase in the Even Start Family Literacy Program "to support family-centered education projects helping parents learn literacy and parenting skills while supporting early childhood education for young children." Of course, parents ought to be involved in their kids' education, but it is a sign of the times—and in this sense at least, Gore is a man of our time—that when educators seek to teach children better, they don't focus on better curricula and teaching methods, but on trying to get parents (many of them not well educated themselves and not fluent in English) to take on subjects with which trained educators are having trouble.

It's odd that Gore talks so much about getting parents more involved with their children's schools rather than with their children, and that he calls for more parental involvement when the children hit school age at the same time that he advocates universal preschool, which would lessen parental involvement during their previous, crucial years of development. A central aspect of his overall approach to education is to fuse the role of parent and school—the better to transfer the blame of poor schooling onto parents. (In similar fashion, he also supports character education, which makes teaching values a job for schools, while parents are stuck with homework assignments and trying to boost their children's academic performance.)

Gore has proposed that "we try something new: parents, teachers, and students should all meet together at the beginning of the year, on the first day of school, to agree upon and sign a strict, fair discipline code." Attendance at the meeting would be mandatory. California Governor Gray Davis—the buttoned-down politician who is a Gore education adviser as well as, he likes to quip, the vice president's "charisma adviser"—had a similar plan when he was campaigning for governor. The California legislature did pass a bill to give $40 million to reward schools that managed to get parents to sign disciplinary contracts. But predictably, the contracts weren't mandatory statewide, as advertised. As newspapers reported during the campaign, there is no way for school districts to enforce a contract requirement if parents don't want to participate. After all, what could they do? Refuse to teach the innocent children?

Bad Schools, Good Politicians

President Clinton vowed to end social promotion in his 1999 State of the Union address. Undeterred by the fact that the federal government has no jurisdiction over local schools, Gore immediately echoed that pledge. Why not? Schools do students no favor when they robotically graduate them year after year when these children perform well below grade level. Also, Americans love the idea of ending social promotion for other people's children.

When politicians like Gore raise this subject, they invariably cite the experience of Chicago schools, which announced an end to social promotion, but also give students a second chance to graduate to the next grade by allowing them to attend summer school, potentially funded by the federal government. Chicago's Iowa Test of Basic Skills scores are up marginally. In 1996, 22.6 percent of third-graders scored above the national norm; by 1998, 25.5 percent of them did. In 1996, 32 percent of sixth-graders scored above the national norm; in 1998, 35.8 percent did. In 1996, 33.5 percent of eighth-graders scored above the national norm; in 1998, 38.8 percent did.

While Chicago's experience seems to have been modestly positive, other school districts have had a different outcome. The Johns Hopkins University Center for Research on Effective Schooling for Disadvantaged Students found in 1993 that summer school for the non-promoted had little or no effect on disadvantaged students. Lorrie Shepard of the University of Colorado found that students who were held back were 20 to 30 percent more likely to drop out of school. Linda Darling-Hammond has warned that dozens of studies show that keeping students back a grade "actually contributes to greater academic failure, higher levels of dropping out and greater behavioral difficulties."

When the Oakland Unified School District—a district that, like most others, always prefers rhetoric to action—implemented its first year of mandatory summer school to end social promotion, more than half of the 14,000 children assigned to the program never showed up. Still, the district allowed the vast majority of truant students to move up a grade anyway, which sent a destructive sign to students who want to skate through the system.

Another symbolic issue for Gore is his oft-repeated goal of having every classroom in America be wired into the Internet by the year 2000, even though there's little evidence to support his contention that computers will enhance student achievement. "Most knowledgeable people agree that most of the research isn't valid," said Edward Mille, former editor of the *Harvard Education Letter*, in the *Atlantic Monthly*. "It's so flawed, it shouldn't even be called research. Essentially, it's just worthless." According to Bill Rukeyser of the nonprofit group Learning in the Real World, "The studies presented by the pro-computer advocates tend to rely on small samples, samples done without control groups or [relying on] largely anecdotal evidence."

While some teachers like the idea of computers in the classroom, others fear that computers, like too much television, are harmful to young minds. They ruin attention spans. Besides, computers can only help students who are literate and use them for their studies, not for video games. The *Los Angeles Times* reported on a local elementary school that had spent $500,000 on computers over six years in the 1990s, yet "changes did not register on the school's test scores."

Nonetheless, this new education fad, with the backing of high-tech businesses that stand to profit from it, has prompted schools to drop art classes, music classes and vocational classes and rush to the computer workstation.

Gore also calls for a "nationwide army of volunteer on-line tutors and mentors, carefully screened for safety and qualifications" to help newly wired schools. This is consistent with his push for college students in the AmeriCorps program to teach children to read, but inconsistent with his call for more teacher training. If trained and specially educated teachers can't teach children to read, how can mentors and college students do it?

Gore's Global Warming Youth

Gore would not be Gore if he didn't fit an environmental agenda into his educational policy.

In *Earth in the Balance,* he proposed a "program involving as many countries as possible that will use schoolteachers and their students to monitor the entire earth daily, or at least those portions of the land area that can be covered by participating nations. Even relatively simple measurements—surface temperature, wind speed and direction, relative humidity, barometric pressures, and rainfall—could, if routinely available on a more nearly global basis, produce dramatic improvements in our understanding of climate patterns." This idea became the GLOBE (Global Learning and Observations to Benefit the Environment) program, funded by the federal government.

The GLOBE program gives a strong and unsettling indication that Gore would place himself on the trendy but wrongheaded side of the reading and math wars. The Teacher's Guide for the GLOBE program admonishes teachers, "There are no right or wrong answers; any response is acceptable." Thus GLOBE teaches science the way new-new-math faddists teach math: telling students there are no wrong answers.

You can tell GLOBE is a dumbed-down science program simply by looking at the "skills" that administrators choose to highlight: "Reflecting," "hypothesizing," "brainstorming," and "increasing awareness of one's own environment." Higher-level skills include "questioning, identifying cause and effect and predicting." "Estimating" is a skill. Being able to calculate a right answer to an equation is not a skill. Activities that don't stand up

140

to objective measurements like uniform tests are skills, which leaves measurement of competence up to the teacher's subjective judgment.

Just as trendy math programs require students to write about math, draw pictures about math and tell stories about equations, GLOBE instructs teachers to make assignments in which students "transform [their scientific observations] into representations—sketches, stories or poems." For example, when students go to the study site where they take temperatures or soil samples, they're also supposed to create "drawings, poems and stories" about what they have experienced.

Boosters contend that these hands-on exercises will show kids what it's like to be a real scientist. If so, the profession comes across as a yawn. Consider GLOBE's "water temperature protocol" for measuring tap water temperature. The teacher's guide suggests, "Have your students work in teams in the classroom to measure tap water temperature, each team using its own thermometer." Then students record their findings. "If there are any abnormal measurements, discuss why they might have occurred." This is when the teacher can discuss data quality, then help students "improve their technique" of measuring water temperature. And: "Continue taking measurements until they are all sufficiently consistent." It is safe to say that not many Cricks and Watsons will be created by this curriculum.

Testgate

In February 1999, the National Center for Education Statistics (NCES) was set to release the scores from the National Assessment of Educational Progress (NAEP), which tests student skill levels by state and nationally. Since the 1998 NAEP scores were

141

up from 1994, Al Gore decided to announce the results, although the vice president's presence was considered bad form by NCES folk who prefer not to politicize their findings. (When President Bush pulled a similar move in 1992, the NCES board chairman objected.)

Nonetheless, Gore insisted on taking credit for the modest gains: "I am proud to report to you new evidence that our efforts are beginning to pay off. For the very first time reading scores have improved for each of the three grades measured by the National Assessment of Educational Progress, fourth grade, eighth grade and twelfth grade. This is great progress and we're proud to report it." Besides President Clinton and himself, Gore praised Head Start, Even Start, the administration's class-size reduction efforts, and AmeriCorps.

There was one little problem: Scores were up from 1994 primarily because they had dropped during the first two years of Clinton and Gore. Compared to 1992 scores, the new NAEP scores were a wash. Fourth-graders were the same as in 1992, eighth-graders scored slightly above 1992 and 1994, twelfth-graders scored over 1994 but below 1992. As *Investors Business Daily* editorialized, "To put these numbers in context, 38 percent of fourth-graders, 26 percent of eighth-graders and 23 percent of twelfth-graders scored below the most basic measure for reading at grade level in 1998—hardly an endorsement of Washington involvement."

Mark Musick, chairman of the National Assessment Governing Board, wrote a letter complaining about Gore's performance. NCES head Pascal Forgione spoke to the *Los Angeles Times* about the inappropriateness of Gore's trying to capitalize personally on the NCES scores. Suddenly, the administration informed Forgione that his four-year appointment would not be renewed. It didn't matter that Education Secretary Richard Riley wanted Forgione to be reappointed or that the Advisory Council on Education Statistics advised that he stay on. Forgione resigned.

Education Department spokeswoman Julie Green denied to the *Austin American-Statesman* staff that the dispute with Gore had anything to do with Forgione's dismissal. (An NCES source told me confidentially that the "Gore connection" was only "one of the reasons" why Forgione got the axe.) Green added that Gore's presence at the press conference was "completely important and obviously appropriate." She said that Forgione was fired because he had tax problems. It's true that Forgione did have a tendency to file his taxes late. He told the *Weekly Standard* he did so as part of a "forced savings" program. He got a refund in all eight years in which he filed late, which he used to pay his children's college tuition. Forgione's late filings were not an issue during his 1995 confirmation hearing; they only became an issue when he crossed Al Gore.

The parallel with the White House Travelgate scandal is unmistakable. In Travelgate, President Clinton had every right to dismiss travel office employees. But the new president and his inner circle didn't want to take any political heat for their decision or come across as crass patronage barons, so they alerted the media that the FBI was investigating travel office staff for criminal misdeeds. To make themselves look better, in other words, Clinton and his loyal staff smeared a bunch of civil servants.

By spreading the word that Forgione was late filing his taxes, the Department of Education got in that little extra dig against a man it was firing. As Christopher Caldwell wrote in the *Weekly Standard,* the Forgione case reveals "the sign of a bizarre need on Gore's part to disguise his Machiavellian motives from himself."

Start the Revolution Without Him

For all his talk about wanting "revolutionary" change, the last thing you should expect Al Gore to do is cross the teachers' unions by endorsing the truly "revolutionary" proposal—vouchers—that could spell relief for poor children stuck in bad schools. As he said in his first education policy speech in May 1999, "We must reject the false promise of siphoning public school funding away to private schools. That would only make things much worse."

Coyly criticizing Texas Governor George W. Bush's call to give $1,500 vouchers to parents whose children attended poor schools that failed to improve in three years, Gore proclaimed before a group of mostly Hispanic elementary school students in Rhode Island, "Some people have said that if a school is falling behind all the money ought to be taken away and the school should be shut down and the parents should be given a little bit of the money to hire tutors or make a down payment on private schools. I think that would be a disaster." Yet Gore doesn't consider it a disaster if kids spend four years in a school that can't even teach them to read near grade level.

For a man who talks about shaking things up, Gore has a remarkable reluctance to search out programs that really work or to notice when his reforms, pre-blessed by the educational bureaucracy, don't really help students. George W. Bush has been similarly clumsy in trying to position himself as an "education president," but at least he has publicly embraced phonics as a way to insure that every child can read. In 1999, Bush visited Inglewood, California's Bennett/Kew elementary school, where 51 percent of the students are black and 48 percent are Hispanic, and some 40 percent of the children who attend kindergarten are not fluent in English. After switching to phonics, principal Nancy Ichinaga brought her students' reading scores up from the bottom 3 percent to surpass the 50 percent mark. In 1999, Bennett/Kew second-graders scored at the 66th percentile in reading and the 77th percentile in math. While education reformers talk about requiring that all students can read by the end of the third grade, Ichinaga said, "Our children learn to read by the end of the first grade." Adopting the same Open Court phonics system, Sacramento City Unified School District brought first-graders from the 35th percentile nationally in reading to the 62nd percentile in two years, at a cost of about $100 per student, plus textbooks.

Phonics truly is a revolutionary concept in today's educational context, but Al Gore is oblivious to it.

Then there's the Core Knowledge curriculum developed by E. D. Hirsch Jr. at the University of Virginia. The program has been so powerful that it has students at North Carolina's Healthy Start Academy outperforming expectations. The charter school works because of its strong curriculum, tough discipline, prayer at lunch, no teachers' union and high ambitions for all students. Kindergarteners learn about continents and oceans, first-graders about Egypt and Mesopotamian civilizations, second-graders about Asia, and fourth-graders about world history. While 80 percent of Healthy Start students are eligible for free or subsidized lunches, the elementary school scored in the 88th percentile in reading and 91st percentile in math on the Iowa Test for Basic Skills.

Yet Gore's "revolutionary" education proposal doesn't include Core Knowledge.

▲

In presenting himself as a revolutionary while defending the status quo, Gore has said that education "is the greatest anti-poverty program...we could ever have." Certainly this was true of his own education at St. Albans and then Harvard. And it has been true for his four children, who also attended private schools that provide a hedge against poverty. Yet the ability to attend a local parochial school—one without the upper-class cachet of a St. Albans—is beyond the means of America's poor children, many of whom are stuck in public schools that don't educate them and thus consign them to illiteracy and low achievement. And Gore, who has billed himself as an outside-the-box innovator on social issues and committed to affirmative action, is so deeply in hock to the educrats that he has refused to consider any measure to give that opportunity to the children who need it most.

When philanthropists Ted Forstmann and John Walton recently set up an organization to sponsor 40,000 scholarships for students attending failing public schools, they received 1.25 million applications—these from impoverished parents who knew they'd have to come up with $500 to $1,500 of their own money to use these private vouchers. Gore resolutely denies that opportunity to the 1.2 million desperate lower class kids who didn't get those scholarships (children were chosen by lottery), and says he is doing this for their own good. When *Time* magazine's Tamala Edwards asked him how he could deny poor children vouchers after sending his own kids to private schools, Gore would not address her question.

Gore's advocacy of a strict discipline contract between parents and schools doesn't fit with his personal behavior, either. According to *Washingtonian* magazine, he pulled his son from St. Albans after Albert III, then thirteen, was caught "in possession of substances popular among teenagers but banned by the school's honor code." The Gores didn't like the punishment that administrators meted out to their son, so they removed him from St. Albans, then placed him, not in a public school, but in Sidwell

Friends, another private institution for the children of the rich and powerful (including Chelsea Clinton).

CHAPTER SEVEN

Crime and Press Release

Al Gore seized on the hate crime issue after three racist thugs murdered James Byrd Jr., a black man, by dragging him to death behind a pickup truck and after two violent homophobes murdered Matthew Shepard, a young gay man in Wyoming. He told a Democratic gathering, "If James Byrd is dragged behind the back of a pickup truck by bigots because of his race, when Matthew Shepard is crucified on a split-rail fence by bigots, how can any political leader in either party say that there is no difference between hate crimes and other crimes?" He repeats those lines almost verbatim whenever he presses for passage of the Hate Crimes Prevention Act.

In Goredom, perhaps a new federal hate crime law would do more than existing laws to curb racially-motivated murders and assaults. But it is not clear that this is the case in the real world. Surely Texas jurors' decision to sentence two of Byrd's killers to death should serve as a more effective deterrent to homicidal racists than the possibility of federal prosecution. But merely calling for more federal death penalties (which he already supports) would not solidify Gore's standing with three of what campaign manager Donna Brazile calls the "four pillars" of the

Democratic party—women, blacks, and other ethnic minorities (the fourth is labor)—nor with the "emerging" pillar of gays and lesbians. So he calls for another law against hate crimes designed more to inflame the sensibilities of his minority clientele than to punish thugs.

If hate crime laws really made a difference, there would have been no need for a federal law because former Texas Governor Ann Richards had already signed a state hate-crimes bill long before the gruesome murder of James Byrd. But to listen to Gore, you would think no hate crime bills ever have been passed anywhere. In November 1999, he told a group in New Hampshire, "Hate crimes are intended to stigmatize and dehumanize and put fear in the hearts of a whole group of people and I believe it's time to pass a national hate crimes law." Not only does he ignore the Texas law, he also ignores the 1968 Civil Rights Law, which gave the Justice Department jurisdiction to investigate and prosecute crimes based on race, religion or national origin if the crime was committed because of the victim's participation in a federally protected activity, such as voting or serving on a jury. What's more, a new hate crimes law probably wouldn't stop violence against homosexuals when the Hate Crime Sentencing Enhancement Act of 1994, which included "sexual orientation" as a protected victim class, didn't do so. And there was a Hate Crime Sentencing Act of 1990 before that.

Gore's headline-grabbing position on hate crimes is of a piece with the way he has treated issues of crime and punishment generally. It is not an exaggeration to say that in his tenure as vice president, Gore has become the ambulance chaser of national tragedies. Speaking at the National Memorial Dedication for victims of the Oklahoma City bombing in 1998, for instance, the vice president patted himself on the back by saying that he and President Clinton had "worked across party lines" to increase the antiterrorism budget by almost $3 billion.

149

After students Eric Harris and Dylan Klebold cut a murderous swath through Columbine High School in Littleton, Colorado, in April 1999, other politicians—notably the president himself—offered consolation and the nation's prayers. Gore too was on the scene with soothing words and his patented solution: "There are children who are hungering for their parents to become more involved in their schools, and to fill the spiritual void in their lives." Such a statement is at least consistent with his plan for more parental involvement in EduLand, but the question bears asking again: Do children really want their parents more involved with their schools or more involved with *them*? And if parents spend more time at schools, rather than with their children, will it lessen the chances of violence? Who cares, as long as Gore looks as though he cares? As Gore pollster Paul Maslin explained, "I thought Gore's best moment was in the wake of Columbine. I thought he spoke with more eloquence and more credibility. I think there was a stronger tie in Gore emotionally to what was going on. That stems from what unquestionably was a very close knit family."

Gore can be forceful in such situations, for those who aren't offended by his efforts to make political points from other people's pain. On one post-Columbine TV show, Gore suggested that if his plan to combat sprawl and his call for smaller public schools had been enacted, this might have freed up counselors who, in a more intimate campus, might have seen and prevented the alienation and anger that led to the crime. Later, campaigning in the New Hampshire primary, Gore came out in support of a second high school in a New Hampshire city, saying it might prevent another Columbine.

The pop psychology that plays such an important—and largely unnoticed—part of Gore's thought is fully engaged in ceremonial occasions such as the Columbine memorial and in personal appearances that followed. At Littleton he said, "Where there are families that are under stress and are not doing the job as well as they should, then we need to buttress them and supplement them with mentors and with support networks." At a New Hampshire Town Meeting, he called for "more guidance counselors, more psychologists" to halt school violence.

When Gore said these things to Columbine parents, most who heard his remarks no doubt agreed it would have been good if someone had done something. Yet it is also true that both of the killers came from upper-middle-class families who could have afforded psychologists for their sons, each of whom owned a car, one of them a BMW. How far can government reach into the inner lives of its citizens? Does Gore believe the government should provide counseling for families that can buy their son a Beamer? And doesn't it matter to him that one of the boys underwent counseling and anger management class, which apparently didn't work?

It was during the long aftermath of Columbine that Tipper also became elliptically involved in the issue by going public about her fight with depression. Her rationalization: "If we are serious about stopping the violence and helping our children, we as adults need to erase the stigma that prevents our kids from getting the help they need for their mental health." She implausibly denied having discussed with her husband the ramifications of her announcement on the Gore 2000 campaign. Yet the combination of Tipper and Al talking about counseling suggested that if they became First Couple, the governess state would also become a therapeutic state.

In May, weeks after Columbine, Gore went on "Larry King Live" to discuss the crime again. "Larry, I was deeply affected, and I told this story the other day. I thought a long time before I told it," he said, "because it was shared with me in a private moment. Tipper and I went out a couple of Sundays ago and physically embraced the families of all those who died in Columbine High School. And one of the fathers—I won't use his name to protect his privacy, he might not even care, but it was so private. He whispered into my ear during the midst of the embrace, 'These children cannot have died in vain. We have to make some changes. Promise me we'll make changes.' And then he repeated it in a tone with urgency and insistence that went just straight to my heart and my soul. He said, 'Promise me.' And I said, 'I promise,' and I meant it, and anybody would have said the same."

There were eerie echoes in this tale of the other times Gore has publicly gotten up close and personal about his innermost thoughts—in his words about his son's accident and his sister's tobacco-caused death. The only difference was that here he was ransacking others' lives instead of his own family's to gin up emotional effect.

Anti-Gun

Gore's long-range strategy has been to use crime to woo the votes of women, 66 percent of whom want tougher gun laws, according to an Associated Press poll, and 88 percent of whom favor registration of all firearms, according to a Gallup poll. During the primary season, Gore frequently talked about school violence, handgun registration and a ban on some junk guns, framing the crime issue generally as a family issue. In fact, Gore's big crime speech was entitled, "Fight Crime for America's Families."

In the spring of 1999, Gore capitalized on the anti-gun sentiments inflamed by Columbine when he presided over the Senate to cast a dramatic tie-breaking vote in favor of a measure to require background checks at gun shows, mandate safety locks, and ban the import of ammunition clips that hold more than ten rounds. The vote seemed especially urgent because that very day there was a high school shooting in Georgia.

Gore announced, "Now I personally would like to dedicate my tie-breaking vote to all of the families that have suffered from gun violence." And: "This is a turning point for our country."

After all the spectacle and all the posturing that accompanied it, however, his fellow Democrats would end up killing the bill. Democrat Representative John Dingell inserted what became a poison-pill amendment, generally supported by Republicans but opposed by his own colleagues, calling for gun checks to be completed in twenty-four hours instead of seventy-two. House Judiciary Committee Chairman Henry Hyde was so desperate to get the media to report his willingness to negotiate even on those terms that he released a written text of his gun show proposal. It called for completing checks within twenty-four hours, but allowed for three extra business days if there was a need to check further. The big problem, Hyde complained to Reuters, was that every time he tried to strike a compromise, the Democrats would find another reason to make sure it failed.

The Dingell amendment gave the Dems a chance to huffily refuse to vote for the bill and save the issue for the 2000 election. As the *Wall Street Journal* editorialized, "If Democrats really thought gun control mattered, they wouldn't have killed a bill that still tightened regulations on sales at gun shows and mandated safety locks."

After not intervening or pushing Democrats to pass a bill that he said would "make our children safer," Gore took full political advantage of the bill's defeat. Speaking in Los Angeles before a group of high school students, he proclaimed, "There is only one reason the Republican leadership in Congress fought against closing that gun show loophole. It's because of the National Rifle

Association and their gun lobby." He used the issue in October 1999 to the same effect. "The time has come to hold them accountable for not acting," he said. And again in November: "How many tragedies does it take before the members of the Republican leadership bottling up this legislation get the message?"

In June 1999, Gore had argued, "Incredibly, while these eighteen- to twenty-year-olds cannot legally buy a beer, cannot purchase a bottle of wine and cannot order a drink in a bar, right now they can walk into any gun shop, any pawn shop, any gun show, anywhere in America, and buy a handgun." That simply was not true. The Gun Control Act of 1968 prohibited the sale of handguns to anyone under twenty-one. Gore was calling for a new law to do the same thing a thirty-one-year-old law already did. And when he found out that the law already banned handgun sales to those under twenty-one, he didn't bother to rethink his position or call for tougher enforcement of the existing law he had forgotten about.

In March 2000, when a sixth-grader held another student at gunpoint until a teacher convinced the boy to surrender, Gore told the Associated Press that the story signaled the need for more gun-control measures like child-safety locks. But it turned out that the boy's father had used a trigger lock on the gun, and the child had found the key and removed it.

In announcing his crime initiative in July 1999, Gore stuck to limiting registration of new gun purchases, no doubt because he was aware that a third of all American households keep a gun. "As president, I will do whatever it takes to get the guns away from children and criminals, and close every loophole in our law books," he said. "I will fight for a national requirement that every state issue photo licenses for anyone who wants to buy a handgun. Unless you obtain a license and pass a background test and pass a gun safety test, you could not buy a handgun under this law. Not in a gun shop, not at a gun show, not on a street corner, not anywhere in America."

Yet critics question whether new gun laws will have any effect when the federal government has done such a lax job of enforcing existing gun laws. Despite the existence of the Gun-Free School Zones Act, six thousand students were caught at school with guns in 1998–99, but only thirteen were federally prosecuted. The Justice Department prosecuted only five people in 1997 and six in 1998 for violating the ban on juvenile gun transfers. There were no prosecutions for those who broke the Brady Bill law against felons buying guns in 1996 and 1997, and only one prosecution in 1998.

When confronted with these statistics, Justice Department spokesman Brian Steel argued that there has been a 25 percent increase in prosecutions. But since none of this increase has occurred at the federal level, this means that state and local prosecutions are up. And so, if state and local prosecutions are up, why enact more federal laws that will not be enforced?

While the vice president presents himself as an absolutist on gun control, there is a striking similarity between his position on this issue and his "evolved" position on abortion. In both cases, his change of heart—which the Gore Disconnect allows him to deny having had—was calculated to appeal to the broad liberal constituency he needed when his ambitions had outgrown his conservative constituents in Tennessee. When a member of Congress, Gore voted against gun-control measures. In 1985, he opposed a fourteen-day waiting period. He voted to exempt many gun collectors from the Gun Control Act of 1968 and remove the ban on interstate sales of rifles, shotguns and handguns. In fact, Gore voted with the National Rifle Association on all five votes the organization considered critical in the Senate through May 22, 1990. The next day, he suddenly shifted, voting against the

NRA in support of a bill that banned nine assault weapons. Pro-gun through his first presidential campaign and for a time after it, Gore apparently saw the handwriting on the wall of national politics one day and went with the changing consensus. Nonetheless, spokesman Roger Salazar told the Associated Press, "I think the vice president has been very consistent on all these issues."

▲

While Al Gore was saying that parents should combat school violence by spending more time at their children's schools, many other Americans were blaming the entertainment industry for the proliferation of violent juvenile crime because of the way movies and television have inured children to mayhem and video games have allowed them to experience the vicarious thrill of killing and wounding strangers. Some gun owners also noted that if Washington could infringe on their rights, then Gore should lean on Hollywood too.

Gore faced a dilemma. He'd had a dicey relationship with Hollywood from Tipper's Parents' Music Resource Center days, but in the past few years the relationship was definitely on the mend and many big Hollywood Democrats were contributing to his campaign. Yet because of that old self-inflicted wound, Gore had trouble getting away with what Bill Clinton had done: raise money from Hollywood one day, then bash Hollywood the next, with the latter action soon forgotten or forgiven as a necessary exercise in hypocrisy.

In 1999, when Clinton ordered a federal study to be done jointly by the Justice Department and the Federal Trade Commission into the link between the entertainment industry and violence, Gore found himself in the hot seat. If he went against the industry and publicly supported a tough study, contributions and star support might dry up and the Hollywood crowd could defect to Bill Bradley during the primaries. And if Gore sided with the industry, he opened himself up yet again to charges of pandering. So he set up a private meeting with Hollywood movers and shakers who afterwards wouldn't tell the *Los Angeles Times* what he said about the proposed federal study. DreamWorks spokesman Andy Span did tell the paper, "As the vice president has begun to address this issue, I think many in the industry who had concerns have been made more comfortable."

But because he was committed to the idea of government as the solver of all problems, Gore had to present some sort of solution for entertainment violence that went through Washington. As he said in his big crime speech, "I will take on those who deliberately peddle degradation and violence to our children and work for self-restraint in TV and on the Internet, along with the V-Chip and related tools, to guarantee that parents finally get real choices—and real control." You would never guess that in 1998, when Disney, one of Gore's top ten career donors, opposed the Child Online Protection Act which would have imposed criminal penalties for commercial Web sites that recklessly displayed pornography to minors, Gore aide David Beier led a White House team that fought the legislation.

During the Columbine hangover, Gore revisited the issue: "When it comes to the Internet, too many parents now feel like they're faced with a false choice, between unplugging that computer in the family room or spending every single moment looking over their child's shoulder to make sure they're not wandering into some dangerous online alleyway." But there was, said Gore, a third way: the Parents' Protection Page, which would serve as a sort of yellow page for parents that also allows them to block or monitor what their children are doing on the Internet. Gore once again cited the anonymous Columbine parent who made him promise there would be changes. And then, pointing out that the Parents' Protection Page would be online in July, he said: "Now that's action and that's speed."

But while Gore made it seem as though the device was a response to Columbine, in fact, the industry and members of Congress, both Republican and Democrat, had been working on the page for some time before the shooting. As Bartlett Cleland of the Internet Education Foundation complained, "There was no Gore involvement. They hijacked this issue."

Before the announcement of this initiative, industry people who had worked on the page protested Gore's flagrant attempt to take credit for a project with which he had not been involved. In a conference call, they also told Gore's domestic policy adviser Jim Kohlenberger that it was wrong to leave out Republicans who had worked on the project, and threatened a boycott. In response, Kohlenberger threatened the techies, saying, according to the *Washington Times*, "If you do not show up, [Gore] will notice, and he has a very long memory for these things."

Carrying a Small Stick

Gore's tough-on-crime talk turned to embarrassed silence when President Clinton proposed to grant clemency to sixteen convicted Puerto Rican terrorists in the summer of 1999. These prisoners had not been convicted of the bombings themselves, but had served nineteen years on charges that included armed robbery, sedition, interstate transportation of firearms with the intent to commit a crime and interference with interstate commerce by violence. The FALN, Spanish acronym for the Armed Forces of National Liberation, had staged some 130 bomb attacks in the United States from 1974 to 1983, in which six people died—for a cause, independence, that Puerto Ricans have rejected at the ballot box. The Federal Bureau of Investigation, the Federal Bureau of Prisons, U.S. Attorneys in Illinois and Connecticut, and a Department of Justice pardon attorney all had opposed clemency. The sixteen convicts had not even petitioned for it, because to do so would have been to recognize the authority of the U.S. government. To qualify for this act of mercy, they had to renounce violence. Two FALN convicts refused that condition, and therefore the clemency offer.

The *National Journal's* legal columnist, Stuart Taylor Jr., noted that Clinton had been a hard-nose when it came to clemencies generally, having granted them only 111 times out of 3,229 requests, or 3.4 percent of the time, "the lowest percentage granted by any President since the government started keeping clemency statistics in 1900." Former Clinton political consultant Dick Morris wrote that he was convinced the move was an attempt to woo the New York Puerto Rican vote for Hillary Clinton in her then unofficial bid to be elected to the U.S. Senate from New York. The White House denied the charge. Hillary Clinton, nonetheless, came out against the clemency move, saying that the convicts had failed to show sufficient contrition. Then, when that tack didn't work to her electoral advantage, the first lady recanted and supported her husband's decision, with the explanation that "the consultation process was not what it should have been."

A memo surfaced in November 1999 that suggested Clinton actually may have been trying to woo those Puerto Rican votes more for Gore than for his long-suffering wife. Five months before the clemency was announced, Jeffrey L. Farrow, co-chairman of the White House's interagency working group on Puerto Rico, wrote a memo to Deputy Chief of Staff Maria Echaveste in which he called for a resolution of the clemency issue, noting, "The VP's Puerto Rican position would be helped." Farrow also noted that the issue was important to three important Puerto Rican lawmakers, New York Representatives Jose Serrano and Nydia Velasquez, and Luis Gutierrez of Illinois. When Echaveste forwarded the memo, she added an e-mail message to Charles

Ruff, the White House counsel who eventually recommended clemency, "Chuck—Jeff's right about this—very hot issue."

White House spokesman Jim Kennedy insisted that neither Gore nor his staff had anything to do with the decision. Yet as Republican National Committee chairman Jim Nicholson pointed out, staff talking points written for Gore showed that he was aware that the clemencies were under consideration and that he likely discussed them with Puero Rican political leaders.

The story provided the RNC with many opportunities to rib the vice president. Jim Nicholson pulled out a 1996 quote from a Gore talk to victims of terrorist bombings: "If you plot terror or act on those designs, within our borders or without, against American citizens, we will hunt you down and stop you cold." He called on Gore to take a stand on the clemency question. But Gore refused. Despite his tough campaign talk about both terrorism and crime, the vice president argued that "The proper course of action is to wait to review the analysis now underway that will be presented to the White House later this week and I'll defer judgment until that time." For this crisis, Gore did not visit families of the victims or promise to make sure the victims did not die "in vain." And weeks later, Gore still had not made his position clear, although a vice chairman of Gore's Puerto Rican presidential campaign told a local paper that the vice president "expressed his support for the clemency."

Toward the end of September, NBC's Matt Lauer asked Gore on the *Today* show if the clemency decision was a good one, and Gore still couldn't give a straight answer. "Well, you know, that's one of the few parts of the Constitution where a power is given to the president without any checks and balances, no oversight or review by the Congress, and it's always a very personal decision that I know that is made after a careful review of the record. I haven't seen the record. In light of the whole deal, I'm not going to criticize or second guess."

Later, when asked about this comment in which he seemed to be saying that he wanted to review the documents and then pass judgment on Clinton's decision, Gore told the *New York Times*, "There may be a misunderstanding. What I meant was that at that moment, the White House was in the process of reviewing its decision-making. I have not reviewed the records, and here's why: This is a power given to the president, without any checks or balances. It's not reviewable by anyone."

In November, the House Government Reform Committee issued findings on the brouhaha, concluding that the White House saw "political benefit" from releasing the terrorists, and that the original FALN sentences were fair, and that those offered clemency were "violent offenders." The Committee was most troubled by the fact that Clinton aides "seemed to want clemency more than the terrorists," citing the fact that it was a White House working group that thought to prompt former President Jimmy Carter to write a letter in favor of clemency. Also, one White House staffer frequently called the convicted terrorists "political prisoners."

Gore might have found this a difficult issue on which to take a stand, but other politicians did not. Senate Democrats and Republicans voted 95–2 for a resolution condemning the clemency decision. The House voted 311–41 to condemn the move. Chicago's Democratic Mayor Richard Daley protested, "It was wrong then. It's wrong today. I don't care who it is…they have no right to plant a bomb in front of your home."

Representative Rod Blagojevich (D-Ill.) told the *Chicago Tribune*, "Vice President Gore should step up and renounce [the clemency deal]. Why would it be difficult for him? He wants to be leader of the country. He should show less profile and more courage."

161

CHAPTER EIGHT

An Evil in the Human Soul

What Ward Connerly remembers most about meeting Al Gore is the vice president's handshake. The date was December 19, 1997. President Clinton had been taking heat because his panel on race relations, which was supposed to create a "dialogue," had rigorously excluded views contrary to those of the administration. Panel chairman John Hope Franklin had said that Connerly—a black University of California regent and the high-profile advocate of Proposition 209, the 1996 voter-approved initiative that ended racial and gender preferences in California state hiring, contracting and college admissions—had "nothing to contribute" to the panel. To quell public criticism that the dialogue on race was actually a monologue in disguise, the White House finally set up a meeting between Clinton, Gore and nine opponents of racial preferences, including Connerly, scholars Abigail and Stephan Thernstrom, Linda Chavez of the Center for Equal Opportunity, former Peace Corps Director Elaine Chao of the Heritage Foundation and GOP Representative Charles Canady (R-Fla.).

As Jim Sleeper later described the event in the *New Republic,* Clinton used the meeting as an opportunity to try to co-opt the opposition, but Gore wanted "to wield moral reproach as a means of discrediting opponents of affirmative action.... Gore repeatedly misconstrued their comments as positions they don't really hold and lectured them about racist evils which some of them know more intimately than he does." Sleeper's characterization fit with biographer Bob Zelnick's definition of Gore's attitude toward opponents of race and gender preferences: "Like scientists who question global warming, they had become wicked heretics who merit excommunication from the church of the righteous."

After Connerly and the others made their case that racial preferences were un-American and morally unjust, the vice president finally spoke up. Purporting to address Clinton, not the others, he said, "Could I ask you a question, Mr. President?" He then went on,

> *If you lived in a community that was 50 percent white, 50 percent black, and for a variety of historic reasons the level of income, educational attainment, and so forth was lower among the blacks in the community, and the police force was 100 percent white, and the problems of the kind that we all deplore took place and other problems took place, and the community decided that the police force would be better able to do its job if blacks were much more represented on the police force, because then the police force would have a much greater ability to relate to the community effectively and to do its job—under those circumstances, do you think that the community would be justified in making affirmative action efforts to open up a lot more positions on the police force for blacks?*

Linda Chavez replied, "With all due respect to the vice president, the example he gave, I don't think you could find me a concrete example of such a place in urban America today." Abigail Thernstrom argued that, according to Gore's own logic, affluent white communities that felt more comfortable with white police

163

officers could discriminate against qualified blacks for similarly benign reasons.

Gore didn't respond to Chavez or Thernstrom. (Connerly later said that he felt the vice president was thinking throughout the meeting, "You are evil people with this notion of colorblindness.") Gore also did not respond when Representative Charles Canady said that no one present was suggesting the abandonment of outreach programs that target minorities and poor Americans or even saying that racism no longer exists, just that "it is inherently pernicious for our government to classify people on the basis of their race."

Instead, Gore condescendingly argued that affirmative action is necessary because there is a "persistent vulnerability to prejudice—rooted in human nature, prejudice based on race and ethnicity—and other characteristics as well." And he added, in what was to become a stock phrase: "That evil lies coiled in the human soul and all of us face spiritual challenge throughout our lives. And I think that racial differences can serve as a trigger for unleashing hatred."

Participants at this meeting were struck by the fact that Gore would not consider the negative effects of preferences on minorities, even when they were voiced by individuals whose own minority status might be assumed to give their thoughts particular force. They were irked most of all by the vice president's snide implication that unlike him, preference opponents didn't care about minorities—even if they, unlike Gore himself, had experienced racial discrimination first hand.

Thus Gore never really absorbed Elaine Chao's moving story. "I came here as an immigrant," she told the group.

> *I didn't speak a word of English. I came when I was eight years old. My father held three jobs. I learned English at night, after 11:00 p.m., when he came back from work. And that's how I learned English.*

And imagine what it's like not to speak English, and then arriving here and two months later having all these little monsters and goblins ring at your door bell and stick something in your face to get candy. It was Halloween. We didn't know that. But what kept us through those days was—what kept us through those days, you know, was a sense of empowerment that I think you [President Clinton] and the Vice President want for Americans, and that you want to empower people, but you can't empower people by these artificial programs that occur too late. What held my family and me together during those very, very hard times is, we just knew we would never be in this condition forever.

He also seemed not to hear Linda Chavez when she said,

I have to tell you, I resent it deeply as a Mexican American woman that—as the mother of three sons, that my children are assumed not to be able to make it under the same standards as your children. And I just don't think that it is right. And it does something that is very corrosive to minorities to be telling them we don't expect you to meet the same standards.

Gore responded by changing the subject.

"I'd like to say something else, Mr. President," he said. "I dis-agree with what I've heard here, but it's a great learning oppor-tunity and I think the dialogue validates the president's decision to invite all of you to come into the Oval Office." Then, unable to sustain this tenuous note of amity, he went after Connerly again, telling him "It is naive in the extreme to assert that there is no persistent vulnerability to prejudice." He continued to needle Connerly for not including children of alumni in his ban on racial and gender-based preferences in college admissions.

The final insult did not become clear to Connerly and the other guests until after the meeting, when they found out that unbeknownst to them, the entire conversation had been taped. Thus, Clinton and Gore were at a distinct advantage in this "candid" discussion because they knew their remarks would be heard by the public, while the others thought they were speaking for the president and vice president alone. They were surprised when the White House made the unusual move of releasing a transcript of the talk after the meeting.

But for Ward Connerly, what was said was not the most memorable part of the meeting. As everyone was filing out, Connerly later told me, "Gore walked up, grabbed my hand and crushed it, just shook it like he was going to crush me, you know, with a kind of smile on his face. And I came from that meeting thinking that Gore is a mean SOB, that he is a really mean-spirited guy who doesn't tolerate difference very easily. Nothing that has happened since then alters that point of view."

Introducing Willie Horton

Although he now poses as a defender of black Americans, Gore has not always felt the passion about white racism that he displayed so theatrically in this White House meeting. In fact, he was an early practitioner of the strategy Bill Clinton made into a pivotal moment in his 1992 campaign when he dissed Sister Souljah, the black rapper who had said, "If black people kill black people every day, why not have a week and kill white people?" In challenging the decision of his main challenger, Reverend Jesse Jackson, to invite Souljah to participate in a youth roundtable before the Rainbow Coalition, Clinton boosted his posture as a moderate Democrat not afraid to take on tough issues of race, and positioned himself as a centrist for the general election.

Then-Senator Al Gore had already walked down that road

when he tried to win the nomination with a similar strategy in 1988. At one point during the primary campaign, Gore attacked frontrunner Michael Dukakis for refusing to say why he would be a better president than their common opponent Jesse Jackson. "He's scared to death," Gore said of Dukakis to the *New York Times*. "He's very uneasy with the whole subject [of race]. It's just ludicrous. He is absurdly timid when it comes to uttering even the slightest sound that might somehow be interpreted as containing an unfavorable view of one of Jesse Jackson's positions." Gore said Dukakis's reticence was "patronizing" and "a subtle form of racism," and he added, "If the country is going to mature to the point where we are colorblind and see candidates in terms of their ability and leadership, then we must be prepared to engage in the rough and tumble of politics." Note that in 1988 Gore believed colorblindness was a virtue, while in the late 1990s, in his appearances before black audiences, he regularly ridiculed those who aspired to a colorblind society.

Gore also told reporters in 1988 that advisers had told him not to criticize Jackson, but he bravely had refused to heed their advice. "I've got to include him. Why? It's another form of racial separation. So I have treated Jesse Jackson the same as any other candidate." The subtext of these remarks was clear: Jackson was black and represented interests most white voters didn't share, and those white voters should look to someone like Gore who wouldn't be afraid to take on black leftists.

As Gore was battling to win the pivotal New York primary in 1988, he secured the endorsement of then–New York Mayor Ed Koch. Acting as Gore's surrogate, Koch quickly announced that Jews would have to be "crazy" to vote for Jackson. Gore "sat silently while Koch polarized the city on racial lines," the arch–racial polarizer Al Sharpton later charged. Black audiences got the picture. At one New York debate, Gore talked about his distress at seeing "whites only" signs in the South, causing Jackson supporters in the audience to snicker. "I don't know what's so funny," a clueless Gore responded.

In 1988 Gore also introduced the specter of Willie Horton into American politics. A convicted black murderer whom Massachusetts corrections officials, under Governor Michael Dukakis, had mistakenly furloughed, Horton raped a woman while he was free. Gore dredged up the case and mentioned the furlough program and crimes committed by furloughed convicts during a New York debate, asking Dukakis, "If you were elected president, would you advocate a similar program for federal penitentiaries?" Gore never mentioned Willie Horton by name, but a GOP operative sitting in the audience was struck by the story and decided to look into it. Later on, when the Republicans used Willie Horton against Dukakis during the 1988 general election, the Bush campaign would be accused of racial demagoguery, although it was only following up on a hint supplied by Al Gore.

As vice president, Gore, who had seen the cachet Bill Clinton gained from his closeness to blacks, made a point of speaking at black churches, adopting a Jesse Jackson–like cadence, citing scripture and broadcasting his anguish about white guilt and black suffering. Yet privately, he was a good deal less passionate than the tub-thumping speeches implied. When Clinton nominated Lani Guinier as Assistant Attorney General for Human Rights, Gore was opposed from the start. He thought Guinier's law review articles—which, among other things, singled out for praise "authentic" black leaders who are "politically, psychologically and culturally black"—made her confirmation highly unlikely. As Elizabeth Drew wrote in *On the Edge*, the White House let out the story that Gore had "confronted" Clinton and told the president to read Guinier's writings. Then, as Clinton struggled to defend his choice, Gore asked a list of questions:

"Whether her views reflect your own; whether you think she'd be injured in a confirmation process and this would affect her effectiveness; whether you think that, in the job, she would be a lightning rod for attacks on the administration." After that, according to the spin, Clinton dropped her.

In his book *All Too Human,* George Stephanopoulos writes that Gore, as head of the Reinventing Government initiative, tried to end the racial and gender preferences for federal contractors which he so adamantly supported in the taped White House meeting with Ward Connerly. Stephanopoulos writes that he fought Gore on the subject, Gore won the battle, but the plan to curtail preferences "eventually died a bureaucratic death." When Bill Bradley brought up this passage from Stephanopoulos' book during a debate with Gore in Harlem in February 2000, Gore did not deny that he had tried to get rid of preferences, but responded that "there was no change" in government procurement. But of course, that is what Stephanopoulos had written.

"The Clinton administration has gotten worse on this issue over time," says Roger Clegg, vice president of the Center for Equal Opportunity and an opponent of preferences.

> *Clinton ran as a New Democrat. He dumped Lani Guinier, stood up to Sister Souljah, but he appears to be worse and worse on this. In that respect, Gore reflects the odyssey of the Clinton administration, which has become demagogic on this issue. And that may be a reflection on the fact that the administration has become more embattled with the various Clinton administration scandals. The administration has really had to go to the well of its political base a lot and particularly to groups like the NAACP and the civil rights establishment for support during impeachment. You can see a political explanation for why the Clinton administration has moved to the left on this issue.*

After Monica Lewinsky became a household name and Clinton

needed all the friends he could get, black voters rallied to support the president. Clintonites fanned the ardor of African Americans by inserting race into the perjury issue. Gore himself implied that supporters of impeachment inclined toward racism when he appeared on Jesse Jackson's CNN talk show. Jackson asked him if the president's support for "racial reconciliation" was behind "anti-Clinton mania." Gore responded, "President Clinton and I have been trying to bridge the historic divide that has come about because of race and ethnicity in this country, elevate the role of women in our society, and bring about some other changes— lifting the poor—that have caused many to feel a little unsettled as old patterns begin to give way."

In November 1999, the man who a decade earlier prided himself on his readiness to take on Jesse Jackson paid court to New York's Al Sharpton, who had parlayed racial demagoguery into a kingmaker's position in liberal New York politics in the aftermath of the trumped-up Tawana Brawley affair, in which he had joined the young black woman in falsely accusing white police of assaulting her. Bill Bradley already had courted Sharpton, and so Gore had to follow suit. But his aides tried to stage the meeting behind the backs of the press, failing to tell journalists about the visit beforehand. The press might never have known that Gore and Sharpton were having a tête-à-tête if it had not been held at an apartment across the street from ABC.

Later, Gore would meet privately with Sharpton again, this time at the apartment of his daughter Karenna Gore Schiff. But once the New York primary was secured, Gore began to distance himself so as not to give too inviting a target to the GOP nominee. In a March 2000 debate in Harlem, when CNN's Jeff Greenfield compared Gore and Bradley's meetings with Sharpton to Republican candidates' failure to speak out against the Confederate flag flying over the state capitol in South Carolina, the vice president's four-part response was vintage Gore. First he said that he condemned Sharpton's inflammatory rhetoric. Second, he said that "in America we believe in redemption and the capacity of all our people to transcend limitations that they have made evident in their lives in the past." Third: "I did not meet with Rev. Sharpton publicly." And fourth, while he and Sharpton did discuss "some of the concerns that I have," he would of course "not violate the privacy of that conversation."

Translation: Gore had decided he had the primary sewn up and wouldn't be needing Al Sharpton for a while. He also didn't need to pander to black voters anymore. After his crude treatment of Ward Connerly for pushing for an end to government racial and gender preferences, after months of denouncing those who advocated color-blind policies as defenders of the unlevel playing field, suddenly at the Harlem debate Gore felt the need to disclose that he opposed quotas. "And I would vote against quotas every time they're put up," he said. Quotas: a word that had been missing from Gore's lexicon for months had made a comeback—just in time for the general election.

Gore's Glass House

Gore's ideas about race in America appear to stem in large part from his unique upbringing and the world view it created. Appearing before Unity '99, a national convention of minority journalists, the vice president asked a rhetorical question: "If a young African-American or Latino child graduates from college, wants to become an entrepreneur in this new innovation economy and has a great idea, how do you raise the capital?" Then he gave a rhetorical answer: "In a majority family, I'll tell you what the first move is: Pick up the telephone and call a member of the family and start working that network to find some capital that can be invested."

This was indeed the case with Gore himself. When he started out, all he had to do was pick up the phone and call his father, the ex-senator, who called Armand Hammer or some other wealthy crony if needed, and magically he was set up with a farm and a contracting business and whatever else he needed. Certainly in his lifetime, family connections have opened doors for the vice president at places like the *Nashville Tennessean,* as well as when he ran for office in Tennessee and had to raise money. Membership in a political dynasty gave Gore an inside position on the political fast track.

At the December 1997 meeting with Ward Connerly and other racial preference opponents, Gore lectured them, "And I think people are prone to be with people like themselves, to hire people who look like themselves, to live near people who look like themselves." That statement too was certainly true for Gore. His early campaign inner circle was comprised of white men only: Tony Coelho, Ron Klain, Mark Penn, Bob Squier, Craig Smith. It wasn't until he found himself in trouble in the Democratic primary states late in 1999 that he played the diversity card. He quickly promoted then–deputy campaign manager and political director Donna Brazile, thirty-nine, to the post of campaign manager, making her the first black woman campaign manager ever of a major American presidential campaign. Moreover, as Gannett's Deborah Matthis said on CNN a few weeks later, "She is known as a *real* black woman."

When Brazile got her promotion, the *Los Angeles Times* reported, "Gore's choice of Brazile raised some eyebrows in Washington, where she is known for an abrasive, take-charge manner." Of course, you could say the same thing about the lion's share of political operators, including Tony Coelho, but few folks stay in top slots after displaying Brazile's propensity for making offensive comments, some of them with a decidedly racist edge.

Brazile told the *Washington Post* of her need to beat the

"white boys." (It must have been a bitter pill when she asked Gore to let her report directly to him, and was told she would have to report to white boy Tony Coelho.) Then, in a December 1999 interview, Brazile trashed black Republican Congressman J. C. Watts and retired General Colin Powell, saying that Republicans would "rather take pictures with black children than feed them."

There is irony in Brazile's relationship with Gore. As an aide to Michael Dukakis in the 1988 campaign, Brazile attacked the Bush campaign for racism when it raised the Willie Horton issue: "They used every little code word and symbol to package their little racist campaign." Eleven years later, however, she became the campaign manager of the politician who brought Willie Horton into America's political vocabulary. When she was director of field operations for Richard Gephardt's presidential campaign, she belittled Al Gore, saying, "You don't hear party chairmen going around saying, 'Gore, Gore, Gore.'" Yet later, in 1999, Gore commended her before black audiences for having "high energy and real soul."

If Brazile has "real soul," Gore has shown phony soul. In his campaign, he has repeatedly excoriated Republicans for not protesting the waving of a Confederate flag over South Carolina's capitol. What about the bust of KKK founder Nathan Bedford Forrest in Gore's own state capitol in Tennessee? When I asked spokesman Doug Hattaway, he explained that it was a different matter: "The issue at hand here is flying a flag atop of the state capitol that has people rallying in the streets. [Gore] has taken a stand on the issue, while Bush has avoided taking a stand on it altogether."

As the vice president was railing against the Confederate flag, holding forth in black churches and praising his divisive campaign manager, London's *Daily Telegraph* reported that a Florida legislator had complained that the Gore campaign was sending him letters addressed to "Dear Black Elected Official."

That seemed to summarize Al Gore's racial journey from 1988 to 2000.

Slave Rings

Gore's stock speeches in favor of affirmative action include the story about the time when he was eight and his father took him into "a big, old mansion" and led him past the "ornate dining room" and the parlor to the basement, where Gore Sr. "pointed to the dark, dank stone walls—and the cold metal rings in a row. Slave rings."

In the *New Republic*, Jim Sleeper pointed out that this oft-repeated story shows exactly how out of touch Gore is with blacks in the south. When *U.S. News & World Report*'s Roger Simon asked Gore about the slave rings, he answered, "I grew up in Washington, D.C., and in Tennessee, but I think a lot of people who grew up in the South during the civil rights revolution were shaped by it in profound ways. I know that I was." If that were true, wouldn't Gore tell a story about the experiences of a contemporary, a black friend or neighbor, a story with live people in it?

The Gore rap on race invariably includes not only a sentence or two about slave rings, but paragraphs on his father. He told an NAACP audience once that his father's "brave stands [on civil rights] probably cost him his career." Therefore, he went on to say, "I feel a connection to that struggle and to the NAACP in a personal way." He noted that his father was "a United States Senator from the South who had courage"; who had fought against the poll tax in the 1940s; who was one of only two senators who refused to sign South Carolina Senator Strom Thurmond's 1956 Southern Manifesto which called on Southern lawmakers to support states that defied U.S. Supreme Court desegregation orders; and who voted for the Voting Rights Act of 1965.

All true, and to the late senator's credit; but in his efforts to turn his father into a civil rights martyr, the vice president always leaves out the other, more interesting part of the story. Senator Albert Gore Sr. voted against the pivotal Civil Rights Act of 1964, the most important civil rights legislation for black Americans in the twentieth century. Gore Sr. voted for fifteen of the nineteen amendments designed to water down the bill. Moreover, when it was headed for passage, he tried to undermine it by inserting an amendment that would have allowed most segregated schools to continue to receive federal funds. Gore's measure failed 25–74. Even Senator Barry Goldwater (R-Ariz.), who opposed the Civil Rights Act because he feared it would create a "police state," voted against the Gore amendment.

If Al Gore Jr. had given the NAACP the full story of his father's record, he could have made a contribution to racial understanding. He could have admitted that his father had been a good man, but nonetheless a man of his times, blinkered as we all are by prevailing opinion; and that he came to recognize the rightness of breaking down barriers and passing needed civil rights legislation. Instead, Gore condescends to black audiences by inflating his father's civil rights record and suggesting that Al Gore Sr. sacrificed himself for them and that they can repay the family for this act of martyrdom by supporting the father's equally noble son.

▲

In his quest to keep the black vote from Bill Bradley during the Democratic primaries, Gore began stumping against "racial profiling" early in the 2000 campaign. He told the NAACP in April 1999, "I am outraged by recent reports of 'racial profiling.' DWI is a crime in this nation. DWB"—driving while black—"shouldn't be. It is wrong to pigeon-hole and punish innocent citizens on the basis of race." He told the group that the administration was working on a plan to abolish the practice.

Bill Bradley took advantage of Gore's rhetoric on racial profiling to tweak the Veep, telling Jesse Jackson's Rainbow-PUSH convention in August 1999 that if Gore wanted to do something about racial profiling, it should not be all that difficult: "I say, 'Mr. Vice President, why wait? Walk down the hall, put the executive order in front of the president and ask him to sign it.' " Bradley used that line in an Iowa debate as well. Gore was left with no alternative but to lecture Bradley that he had no business telling Bill Clinton how to take care of black voters.

But while Bradley was able to score debater's points, he didn't score much else. For all his passion on the issue of racial injustice, he couldn't match the impressive list of African-American appointments made by Clinton/Gore. The list includes Secretaries of Agriculture, the Army, Commerce, Energy, Labor, Transportation and Veterans' Affairs, as well as Surgeon General, Budget Director, Drug Czar, Chair of the Nuclear Regulatory Commission, Chairman of the FCC, Deputy Attorney General, Deputy Secretary of State, Director of the National Parks Service, Director of Presidential Personnel, White House Director of Cabinet Affairs and Director of Public Liaison.

In addition, the administration stepped up efforts to steer government and private money to civil rights organizations that had been its staunchest defenders. In 1998, for instance, Gore announced a partnership between the Small Business Administration and the NAACP. Any opposition to quotas by Clinton or Gore visibly absent, a White House press release announced that the partnership was part of a plan "to deliver $1.4 billion worth of loan assistance to African American owned firms by the year 2000." Another announcement on NAACP letterhead specified other civil rights groups, some of them with very clear partisan agendas, that would help sort out who gets the money: the National Urban League, the National Black Chamber of Commerce, the National Council of Negro Women, Minority Business Enterprise Legal Defense & Education Fund, Organization for a New Equality, and Phelps Stokes Fund.

As the Center for Equal Opportunity's Roger Clegg noted, "I think it's quite remarkable to have the federal government in a partnership with a political interest group, particularly an economic partnership." Yet the news media reported the story without comment.

The administration also became a staunch defender of the Community Reinvestment Act, which encourages banks to lend to minorities. Too staunch, some would say. In 1999, the *New York Times* reported that the regulators at the Comptroller of the Currency were compiling a list of pro-CRA bankers and working on a list of "CRA success stories." One large bank complained to the Senate Banking Committee that federal examiners had asked it for the names of bank officers whom they could say supported the CRA.

In 1999, the administration also began pushing for a voluntary code among advertisers to place their ads in minority-owned media outlets. As the *Wall Street Journal* editorialized, "It's becoming increasingly clear that a key figure in this strategy of guaranteeing revenue pass-throughs to party members will be Al Gore."

Every element of Gore's courtship of the black vote, such as his emphasis on tokenism and delivering taxpayer money to supporters, has come into play in his courtship of the Latino vote as well. With the Republican party expected to work hard to win Latino votes in the year 2000, Gore is likely to intensify his efforts. Instead of spouting Scripture to Latino groups or using the term "dis" as he frequently does in front of black groups, Gore employs the Spanish that he learned as a teenager. His watchwords in front of Latino groups have been "familia, educacion, amor de patria, communidad, y Dios" (family, education, love of country, community and God). He called Bush's voucher proposal "loco." Instead of the slave ring story, Gore started telling Latino audiences about his new role as grandfather, calling himself "abuelito," little grandfather, to give his speeches a South of the Border flavor. The politician who bragged that his first grandson was born on the Fourth of July told an Hispanic crowd in Houston, "Perhaps my next grandson will be born on Cinco de Mayo."

When asked if the United States should admit more legal immigrants, he answered, "Somos una nacion de immigrantes, y con orgullo," then translated, "We are a nation of immigrants and with a pride." In July 1999 he told CNN that he was prepared to stop using the term "illegal alien" because it is hurtful to Latinos. "I think undocumented immigrants is an awful lot better phrase than illegal alien," he explained. In a move reminiscent of Citizenship USA, Gore announced in March 2000 that the administration would seek to extend amnesty to illegal aliens in the U.S. continuously since 1986, thus creating another pool of "instant Democrats."

When Cuban-Americans, 12 percent of the Florida electorate, rose up to surround Elián González, Gore distanced himself from the Clinton administration's decision to return the boy to Cuba without voicing any particular disagreement or specifying how he himself would handle the case. But in January and again in March 2000, just as Miami was on the verge of erupting over Janet Reno's handling of the case (and polls were showing that the vice president might be competitive in this presumably Republican state), Gore announced that he opposed Department of Justice attempts to return the child to his father and believed custody should be determined in family court. Said Gore, "Elián should never have been forced to choose between freedom and his own father."

Many Democrats were stunned that Gore would distance himself from the administration. But when Clinton/Gore won 40 percent of the Cuban-American vote in 1996, the Democratic ticket won Florida. Still, as eager as Gore was to court the Cuban-American vote, he managed to straddle the issue. Asked repeatedly what should happen if father Juan Miguel González came to "free soil" and demanded his son's return, Gore would not say if Elián should be returned, only that the judge would take the father's plea "heavily into account." A *New York Times* headline observed, "Gore Speaks of Cuban Boy, Repeatedly but Not Clearly."

Then a few days later, in an interview on the *Today* show, Gore said that the boy ought to be returned to his father, yet refused to answer the question, asked three times by Katie Couric, whether Mr. González should be granted custody if he came to the United States. In other television appearances later in the day he implied that if the question of Elián's future were to be decided by family court, custody would probably go to the father, although he now refused to say what he considered the preferable outcome of the case. Watching Gore make what was supposed to be a surgical political strike into a lose-lose case of pandering, a Bush campaign spokesman told the *New York Times,* "When it comes to the future of Elián González, it's becoming increasingly hard to understand what Al Gore believes in or what he thinks should be done."

▲

Gore also saw the importance of Asian-Americans long before they became a power in identity politics. In the late 1980s, when the Asian-American population in Tennessee was so miniscule it didn't rate mention in the *American Political Almanac,* Gore reached out to the newly created Pacific Leadership Council, founded by a number of well-heeled Asian-Americans including

John Huang, Maria Hsia and James Riady—names that later would surface in the fundraising scandals of the Clinton administration. Gore had spent a small fortune running for president in 1988 and he needed money to launch his re-election campaign for 1990. Hsia and the Pacific Leadership Council helped him by garnering campaign contributions and votes from Asian-Americans and Indo-Americans. A PLC fundraiser in California, for example, raised nearly $20,000 for Gore, and Hsia raised money for Gore's Senate effort that passed through the Democratic Senatorial Campaign Committee.

The relationship carried into the Clinton/Gore administration. After their heavy financial lifting, one Asian-American fundraiser bluntly wrote in a memo that the administration might "appoint additional Asians to regional slots in California." When fundraiser Johnny Chung couldn't get a place on a trade mission, he bluntly told the white DNC executive who turned him down, "If you can't help me, isn't there an Asian high up in the Commerce Department?"

He was referring to John Huang, who used his position to advocate looser immigration policies, including a "sibling preference" to admit the brothers and sisters of naturalized citizens, to which Clinton initially had signaled his opposition. And indeed, as the *Boston Globe*'s Michael Kranish reported, in 1996 President Clinton changed his mind and endorsed a "sibling preference" policy one month after Huang raised $1.1 million for the DNC at a fundraiser that cost each participant $12,500. Spokesman Mike McCurry later fumed that it was "outrageous" to associate the fundraiser with the change in Clinton policy.

After the press first reported the activities of Huang and Hsia in 1996, relations between Asian groups and Gore cooled. Senator Dianne Feinstein told the *Los Angeles Times*, Gore "may not have wanted to venture forth" into the Asian community "because of the Buddhist Temple thing." In August 1999, Gore

180

2000 chairman Tony Coelho met with about two dozen Asian-American fundraisers in Los Angeles to do damage control. Long-time fundraiser Mary Miyashita burst into tears and asked whether Al Gore could at least make a courtesy phone call to Huang. Anthony Ching, a Los Angeles lawyer, told the *San Francisco Chronicle* that the DNC "didn't really care about Asian-Americans…. They just took the money and ran."

Ask and Tell

When President Clinton was wavering on his campaign promise to end discrimination against gays in the military, Gore tried to push him not to compromise. Elizabeth Drew, in *On the Edge*, wrote about a conversation in which Gore said it was "a matter of principle." The president should just lift the ban, Gore argued, even though he was sure to be overridden by Congress.

Nonetheless, as a candidate for president, Gore started out on the same page as Bill Clinton. He began his campaign saying that he was in favor of the administration's Don't Ask/Don't Tell policy, although he wanted it to be implemented with "more compassion." It was not until Bill Bradley came out against Don't Ask/Don't Tell—and Gore was facing what he feared might be highly contested primaries in New York and California, in which the gay vote could make the difference—that he changed his position once again and opposed Don't Ask/Don't Tell.

Still, Gore showed he was willing to put blacks before gays in the bloc-vote pecking order when he attacked Bill Bradley for suggesting that the 1964 Civil Rights Act should be rewritten to cover sexual preference. At the 1999 Democratic National Committee convention, Gore warned that opening up the Civil Rights Act could lead to dire consequences by weakening civil rights for racial and ethnic minorities. But when columnist George Will asked Gore on ABC's *This Week* how the Civil Rights Act could be weakened, Gore didn't have much of an answer. "Well, first of all, [gay Massachusetts congressman] Barney Frank opposes opening the act for this purpose," he answered. Then Gore illogically spoke of his support for a law banning discrimination against gays.

Gore had entered the primary hoping that hugs and kisses would serve as stand-ins for the policies he preferred not to support. He had made his share of symbolic gestures, after all. In 1997, he had praised Hollywood for the TV show *Ellen* because "millions of Americans were forced to look at sexual orientation in a new light." He had granted an interview to the *Advocate*, a gay magazine that had been tipped to the fact that "the vice president and his wife, Tipper, have more than a dozen openly gay and lesbian aides on their staffs and count gay men and lesbians among their closest friends and confidants." A staffer apparently leaked the fact that Tipper Gore supports same-sex marriage, causing the *Advocate*'s Chris Bull to ask Gore if the family disagreed on the issue. Gore wouldn't answer. Yet if he wouldn't embrace the full gay agenda, he was still *sooo* sensitive, as when he visited a gay and lesbian center, explaining, "I'm here to learn and also to pay honor to this important organization."

(Despite all of this staged openness, the vice president's campaign manager, Donna Brazile, placed herself in the closet. After years of being out in Washington, the if anything too forthcoming Brazile refused to answer questions about her sexual preference. Stories referred to her not as the first lesbian to manage a major political campaign, but as a "lesbian activist.")

Early in the campaign, Gore refused to take a position on California's Defense of Marriage bill, slated for the March 2000 ballot, which would ban same-sex marriages. He told a gay publication, "I'm going to have to educate myself." Then when Bill Bradley came out against the measure because it was "divisive,"

Gore press secretary Kiki Moore told the *San Francisco Chronicle's* Carla Marinucci that Gore "has said that, if he lived in California, he would condemn this divisive initiative, although personally he opposes same-sex marriage."

The issue of gays in the military caused Gore's first stumble in the twenty-first century. During one presidential debate, ABC's Peter Jennings asked Gore and Bradley if they would have a "litmus test" for members of the Joint Chiefs of Staff requiring them to agree with their call for an end to discrimination against gays in the military. What tripped Gore up was that he had to answer first. Fully expecting Bradley to pander to gays full bore, he tried to preempt him by giving the most gay-friendly answer. "I would insist, before appointing anybody to the Joint Chiefs of Staff, that that individual support my policy," he responded. "And yes, I would make that a requirement." Bradley didn't go for the bait, and Gore was left with the hook in his mouth.

John McCain and other political leaders had a field day with Gore's new position, which would preclude him from nominating some of the most illustrious figures in recent military history.

What to do? Since the leading principle of the Gore Disconnect is never admitting that a change of position has occurred, the campaign held a press conference for what Gore spokesman Chris Lehane termed a "clarification" of Gore's position. The vice president told reporters, "That is not what I meant to convey—that's what you heard." So the fault was with reporters (and the public) for hearing what Gore had said, not with Gore for saying it.

Sister Al

If, as author Toni Morrison has contended, Bill Clinton is America's "first black president," then Al Gore could be considered the first female vice president. Gore's endless attempts to appeal to women voters led *New York Times* columnist Maureen Dowd to quip that Gore tries so hard to identify with women that "he's practically lactating."

When she wrote this, Dowd probably was unaware of a piece written for *Washingtonian* magazine by former Gore Director of Communications Lorraine Voles, revealing that Tipper had taught her all about nursing, Gore himself encouraged her to take Lamaze, and the whole Gore staff was really supportive when she used her breast pump. Whenever possible, Gore surrounds himself onstage with women, notably his "very best friend, my wife, Tipper," his three daughters, and his mother. He even came out in favor of using disposable diapers, despite environmental concerns. "That's not a hard call," he told the *New York Times*. "Global warming is hard, Pampers are easy."

When Gore spoke of his "personal opposition" to abortion at an editorial board meeting at the *San Francisco Chronicle*, he explained, "The reason I don't express it is that I think that the judgment about the choice cannot be made absent an appreciation of the context and the circumstances. An abstract judgment expressed in that way can be completely insensitive to the process of thought and feeling that women bring to that choice, informed by the context and the circumstances in which they make it."

"Al Gore does not speak the language of politics as usual," gushed Representative Grace Napolitano (D-Calif.) in a Women for Gore press release, "he speaks the language of family." This language is something he thinks women particularly speak, and so he says "family" at every opportunity. His crime package is called "Fighting Crime for America's Families." His plan for cancer research is called "Fighting Cancer for America's Families."

"Let's be clear: When we talk about women's issues, we are talking about the issues that touch all of our families, and all of our lives. Women deserve a president who gets that," Gore said in his best just-one-of-the-girls manner at a Women for Gore rally in June 1999. By October, when he was sagging in the polls, Gore started talking about the necessity for the next president to understand the wear and tear on American women. His concern was understandable. As Gore pollster Celinda Lake noted, "We can lose the men and win, but we can't lose the men and women and win."

In a speech to female supporters, Gore said, "Now I'll fight to make this simple principle a reality: you deserve an equal day's pay for an equal day's work." Yet that's not how things necessarily worked in the vice president's own staff. In 1999, *U.S. New & World Report* obtained a copy of payroll records and found that "for every $1 earned by a guy, a woman makes 86 cents. And there's even a difference between those doing the same job. Female staff assistants make 93 cents for every dollar pulled down by the guys."

Even as he was talking like a sister, Gore was hiring like a chauvinist. Susan Estrich, the former campaign manager for Michael Dukakis turned syndicated columnist, catalogued Gore's inner circle in March of 1999: campaign manager Craig Smith, campaign chairman Peter Knight, chief of staff Ron Klain, media adviser Bob Squier, former chiefs of staff Roy Neel and Doug Schoen, foreign policy adviser Leon Fuerth and deputy Treasury secretary Lawrence Summers, as well as kitchen cabinet members, pollster Paul Maslin, former Congressman Tom Downey, and HUD Secretary Andrew Cuomo. No women. "It is extraordinary that there could be a number of very smart people working hard for a candidate, the first Democrat I can remember who actually has a negative gender gap," Estrich quoted a top Democratic woman, "and they still haven't acted to get women around their table."

According to Estrich, only one woman, Elaine Kamarck, was ever considered part of Gore's inner circle, and she left Gore's staff to teach at Harvard's Kennedy School of Government. She was about to join the campaign, but only to work under a man, Christopher Edley, who would head policy. (At the same time, Bill Bradley's much smaller campaign had a female campaign manager and media adviser.)

Gore 2000 later named Marla Romash as deputy chair of the campaign, Kiki Moore as press secretary and Donna Brazile as deputy campaign manager. Still, those were not inner-circle positions. And later, when many of the first group of white males were shown the door, they were replaced by other white males. Chief of staff Ron Klain left. Voilà, white man Tony Coelho was in charge. Media consultant Carter Eskew eased out media consultant Bob Squier. Pollster Harrison Hickman, who like Eskew has worked for big tobacco, replaced pollster Mark Penn. Celinda Lake was hired to help the campaign with women voters, but then let go during the austerity move that caused Gore 2000 to relocate in Nashville. The campaign then hired Lake again when feminist activists complained that Gore wasn't spending enough money on outreach to women—other than blowing $15,000 per month on advice from author Naomi Wolf.

Wolf seemed an odd choice to become a Gore campaign guru. Her first book, *The Beauty Myth,* attacked the cosmetics industry and modern culture for putting too high a premium on glamorous looks, even though Wolf obviously made liberal use of cosmetics to doll herself up. In a later book, *Promiscuities,* she called for "sexual gradualism"—masturbation, mutual masturbation and oral sex—as an alternative to pushing abstinence for teenagers: "If we teach kids about other kinds of sexual exploration that help them wait for intercourse until they are really ready, we let the girl find out her desire...and let kids have an option not to go immediately 'from zero to 60.' Teaching sexual gradualism is as sensible as teaching kids to drive." When Wolf's position as a close adviser became public, Team Gore emphasized that Gore had not turned to Wolf for advice on sex education curricula. Spokesman Chris Lehane told reporters that Gore had not read Wolf's books and that her role was "as an informal message adviser to Generation X."

Wags delighted in wondering what Tipper thought of Wolf's sexual gradualism. The political newsletter *The Hotline* playfully juxtaposed Wolf's sexual gradualism with the lyrics from "Darling Nikki," the Prince song that led Tipper to found her parents' group protesting indecent rock lyrics: "I knew a girl named Nikki. I guess you could say she was a sex fiend. I met her in a hotel lobby masturbating with a magazine."

As Dick Morris wrote in *Behind the Oval Office,* Naomi Wolf had been an unpaid adviser to the Clinton/Gore campaign in 1996. Morris credited Wolf with ideas to help Clinton reach women voters, such as school uniforms, tax breaks for adoption and workplace flexibility. But sources told reporters that her role in the Gore campaign was to advise Gore on his wardrobe. She was credited for Gore's move to khaki suits and earth tones, and for his being more aggressive when he first debated Bill Bradley. "She often said that the candidate who best understood the fatigue of the American woman would win," said Morris—which tells us where Gore got his line, "If you do not understand the fatigue of the American woman, you do not deserve to be president of the United States."

Wolf's most famous theory about how to sell Gore, as *Time* magazine reported, was that "Gore is a 'Beta male' who needs to take on the 'Alpha male' in the Oval Office before the public will see him as the top dog." Or as CNBC's "Hardball" host Chris Matthews put it, Gore clearly had been reduced to "hiring a woman to teach him to be more like a man."

The hiring of Wolf showed, if anything, how little the campaign understood women. One bitter Gore staffer told the *Washington Post,* "She is not my sister. I've been struck by the vitriol, and I think some of it comes from her making no attempts to form bonds or promote other women in the campaign." Worse, it turned out that for months, while Wolf was getting rich, female political activists had been pushing the campaign to hire someone to handle women's outreach, to put on more women's events and engage in more networking with women's activists. But the campaign told them it didn't have the money.

When he was asked about Wolf on ABC's *This Week*, Gore's answers were clearly intended to mislead. He dismissed a question about Wolf's $15,000-a-month salary, saying that Wolf only made "a third of that," without acknowledging that Wolf had indeed earned more than he himself did until Donna Brazile recently cut her pay. Brookings Institution analyst Stephen Hess marveled to the *Sacramento Bee*, "Campaigns can get the Naomi Wolfs of the world free. The idea that they paid her for stuff she would have been thrilled to provide for nothing is evidence of how far the Gore operation has run amok."

What Hess didn't realize is that Wolf had made herself priceless to Gore by excelling at one of the oldest career advancement skills in history: flattery. In a June 1998 column she wrote for *George* magazine, Wolf argued that if Gore could "come to terms with his natural eccentricity," he might be just the right leader for the new millennium. It would be impossible for anyone to write a piece that stroked Gore's increasingly grandiose conceits about himself more masterfully. She lauded Gore's "nerd-visionary instincts." She confessed she was impressed with Gore's call for looking at the earth from space, because he understood that a global view would reveal the parochialism of nationalism. Thus "Gore may have discovered common ground with a generation of voters who are young enough to be his children"—which is why the "elite media dismiss his global Americanism at every turn." Get it: the elite media are jealous of Gore, because "these 'insiders' have the most to lose from Gore's Big Think parlance."

"If he can endure the risk of ridicule (beyond anything else he has yet endured) from elites," Wolf continued, "his 'goofy' positions will have become, in three years' time, the global leadership position." In addition, she saluted Gore's "milk-fed handsomeness" and posited that he "is probably a Blakean deep inside, one of those originals who were born blessed (or perhaps cursed) with a unique ability to see connections between things where others see separateness."

You can picture Al Gore reading this article and thanking the stars that he finally found someone who truly understood him.

As a bonus, Wolf sympathized with the difficulty of being a visionary in an insufficiently appreciative world. "To be that kind of savant when one is a famous senator's son, for whom any overt weirdness would entail a kind of social death, might breed a formidable inner conflict." Not only did Wolf appreciate Gore for his formidable ideas, but she also saw his alleged flaws as part of the cross he was forced to bear. "It must take a toll to act normal when one doesn't feel normal (which may explain Gore's famously flat public speaking style)."

Yes, Naomi Wolf saw what all the slick consultants who were trying to change him had missed: His problem wasn't that he's too dull, but that he's too brilliant. Naturally, Gore decided that Wolf belonged on the payroll and that it would be wrong to nickel-and-dime someone with such a keen appreciation for a man's Blakean side. Here was a *real* woman.

CHAPTER NINE

Solicitor in Chief

Al Gore's Watergate came on April 26, 1996. A high school band heralded the vice president's arrival at the Hsi Lai Temple in Hacienda Heights, California. Two seasoned political fundraisers, Maria Hsia and John Huang, greeted Gore at the entrance along with Democratic National Committee chairman Don Fowler and Democratic Congressman Bob Matsui. Gore received a flowered lei. After meeting with the temple's Venerable Master, Hsing Yun, Gore made a flower offering to the temple's Buddha shrine.

Reporters were barred from the event. Some had questioned the propriety of holding an event at the temple, but Hsia told them she had checked with the White House and was told that it was not a problem to have the luncheon at the temple dining hall.

Gore sat at the head table with the Venerable Master, Hsia and others. Fowler and Matsui spoke a few words before the gathering. After lunch, Gore left to catch a flight to San Jose where he would attend another fundraiser.

But he left behind him no zen-like serenity. For one thing, the event at that point had only netted about $45,000, an amount Democratic National Committee officials considered disastrously low considering that White House aide Harold Ickes had anticipated it would bring in $325,000. DNC finance director Richard Sullivan—now a fundraiser for Gore 2000—told John Huang, who had left a job in the Commerce Department to raise money for the DNC from Asian-Americans, "We need you to get some money in." Sullivan expected that since Huang, Hsia and others had pushed so hard to get Gore to the temple, "we would get a big contribution out of somebody"—and he told Huang as much.

Huang got the word out to Hsia, who called the temple's administrative officer, Man Ho, who in turn contacted another nun, temple treasurer Yi Chu, with information that they would have to produce $55,000 more in contributions to meet goals set for the event. Yi Chu, with checkbooks in hand, approached eleven nuns and asked each to write $5,000 checks to the Democratic National Committee, then laundered the contributions by reimbursing them. As the Senate Government Affairs Committee chaired by Senator Fred Thompson later concluded in its investigation, the event total had reached $100,000: $35,000 in donations solicited ahead of time by Temple monastics, $10,000 in laundered donations by anonymous devotees before the vice presidential luncheon, and $55,000 in laundered donations in response to Huang's request for more funds just after the event. According to Thompson, this donation-laundering "clearly violated federal election laws barring political contributions made through 'straw donors' and meets the legal definition of 'criminal conspiracy.'" In addition, at least two of the donors were foreign nationals barred by law from giving to U.S. political campaigns.

There was an even bigger problem with the event. The DNC's Richard Sullivan had warned Huang, "You can't do a fundraiser at a temple," because the temple's nonprofit status prohibited it from engaging in political activity. Violating that law could force the order to lose its tax-exempt status. But then, in the swirl of events that followed, the warning got lost.

191

In October 1996, when the story first broke, Gore immediately set about trying to convince the press that he didn't know the event was a fundraiser. He told National Public Radio's Nina Totenberg, "It was not billed as a fundraiser. It was billed as a community outreach event, and indeed, no money was offered or collected or raised at that event." Then, in January 1997, after the *Boston Globe* reported that a Gore aide had told a reporter that the temple event was indeed "a fundraiser," the vice president changed his story. He said he thought it was a "finance-related" event. Two weeks later, Gore told NBC's *Today*, "I did not know it was a fundraiser. But I knew it was a political event and I knew that there were finance people that were going to be present, and so that should have told me, 'This is inappropriate and this is a mistake; don't do this.' And I take responsibility for that. It was a mistake."

The Senate Government Affairs Committee didn't buy that account. There had been too many staff advisories that mentioned it was a fundraiser. When Gore's deputy chief of staff David Strauss, for example, talked about the event with Huang, his notes included the entry, "John Huang...lead to a lot of $." Two people present at the event had told the committee that someone had talked about fundraising from the podium. The committee's majority report noted, "It will be obvious from the evidence recounted herein that despite various denials, the vice president was well aware that the event was one designed to raise money for his party."

What's more, key evidence was missing. When the story broke, Man Ho and Yi Chu panicked and began destroying documents that they considered "embarrassing." Their story makes for a frightful image: two Buddhist nuns furiously purging paperwork on event preparation, check request forms and the list of attendees in order to thwart any investigation. The nuns testified that no one ordered them to destroy or discard the documents in order to shield an American vice president. The Venerable Master issued a statement asserting that the document purge had "nothing to do with destruction of evidence."

Most suspicious of all was the order's sudden decision to send all videotape footage of the luncheon—including speeches made by Gore and others—to Taiwan, after which the tape conveniently vanished. In addition, the monk who took the tape from the production company left the order and disappeared shortly after the committee issued a subpoena for the videotape. Certainly if the tape supported Gore's version of events, the order would have done all that was necessary to bring it to the committee. Instead, as the Thompson Committee report noted, "Despite the repeated assurances of Temple officials that they are looking for this missing tape—and despite the fact that Temple officials have used short excerpts from this tape in making a brief publicity video that appeared on Cable News Network—the full videotape record of the event with Vice President Gore on April 29, 1996 remains hidden to this day."

▲

When the Buddhist Temple story first broke, some observers felt sorry for the vice president. They figured that squeaky-clean Al Gore had been dragged into the ethical black hole where Bill Clinton lived. That's because they didn't realize that Gore knew Maria Hsia and John Huang long before the Temple fundraiser or that Hsia and Huang had been Gore benefactors since the late 1980s.

Born in Taiwan in 1951, Hsia first entered the United States in 1973 on a student visa. She became a U.S. citizen in 1986. Although not a lawyer by training and lacking even a college degree, she made her living working in immigration law firms, mostly helping Taiwanese citizens to come to the United States. Hsia reported her income as $637,000 in 1982, her best year. In

1983 she earned $449,000; in 1986 she made $362,000. She did well enough to buy a Rolls Royce and a home in Beverly Hills.

Hsia began using political connections to help her clients in difficult immigration cases. She was able to get California Senator Alan Cranston and Representatives Mel Levine, Howard Berman and Harry Reid to write letters to the IRS in her behalf. In return, she mined the Asian-American community for campaign contributions. Hsia's connections also "helped her cultivate an image of a 'connected' political 'player' who could 'make things happen' for her clients," according to the Thompson Committee.

In 1988, a group including Hsia, John Huang, James Riady (whose father Mochtar Riady of Indonesia ran the infamous and powerful Lippo Group), and others established the Pacific Leadership Council. Bankrolled largely with Riady money, the PLC's goals included getting senators to visit Indonesia, Hong Kong and Taiwan with the PLC as host, and getting federal agencies and Democratic Party committees to deposit money in Asian-American banks and provide assistance for "special, exceptional immigration cases."

In 1989, PLC founders decided to send a delegation with five senators and fifteen PLC leaders to Taiwan, Indonesia and Hong Kong. All of the U.S. senators they invited turned the PLC down—except for Al Gore, who would be facing what he feared would be a tough 1990 re-election bid after his unsuccessful presidential run. Financially and psychologically drained, and about to enter his "midlife crisis," Gore told Hsia he would like to get to know the Asian community better. Hsia wrote in a memo that Gore was "willing to work with us on a long-term relationship for his future presidency."

Gore went to Taiwan with wife Tipper, aides Peter Knight and Leon Fuerth, Hsia, James and Aileen Riady, and John and Jane Huang. He toured the Hsi Lai order's Kiaoshung Monastery on January 11, 1989, and there met the Venerable Master Hsing Yun for the first time. The Venerable Master later recalled that when he told Gore, "You can become the president of the U.S.," Gore got excited. He then told Gore, "I will visit you when you become the president."

Hsing Yun jumped the gun by visiting him at the White House in March 1996. Gore called Hsia before the visit to make sure that the Venerable Master wouldn't use the meeting to broadcast Gore's tacit support of Yun's chosen candidates in the upcoming Taiwan election. Instead, Hsing Yun invited Gore to the Hsi Lai Temple for what became the ill-fated fundraiser, and afterward had his order put out a brochure describing the Venerable Master as an "informal liaison to the White House on Asian affairs."

The title really belonged to Maria Hsia. She had earned it over the years by helping organize Asian-Americans and Indo-Americans in Tennessee for Gore, and by getting the PLC to sponsor a $250-per-person fundraiser for Gore in California in 1989. She raised $29,500 for the Democratic Senatorial Campaign Committee, money that was earmarked for Gore's re-election campaign.

Gore repaid the favors. When Congress was working on what was to become the Immigration Act of 1990, he allowed Hsia to lobby him into becoming a co-sponsor of a "family-unity" provision that enabled her and others in her line of work to use one legal resident to leverage the entry of his entire family into the United States. In addition to family-unity language, that Act included provisions for "investor immigrants"—who won visas by creating jobs in America—and for religious workers. The Hsi Lai Temple later paid Hsia to help procure visas for monastics and devotees. Hsia's ties got her a seat next to Immigration and Naturalization Service head Doris Meissner at a 1996 fundraiser, and

195

a photo of herself with Meissner, which no doubt impressed her clientele.

Gore wrote to Hsia to thank her for her "very good counsel." In another note, he wrote, "You are a wonderful friend." Hsia reciprocated, giving Gore an "A" in her personal rating of the responsiveness of members of Congress.

Hsia's advice went beyond immigration law. She also helped Gore with research on Buddhism for *Earth in the Balance*. "He would have been lost without your efforts because the chapter on religion and the environment is integral to his work," Gore's chief of staff Pete Knight wrote to her in March 1991.

Hsia also helped in other ways. The Thompson Committee reported that she and John Huang were "involved in similar donation-laundering as early as 1993." Hsia arranged for three Temple nuns to write checks to the DNC totaling $5,000 and Huang made $45,000 worth of laundered donations. At about that time, Huang escorted Shen Jueren, chairman of China Resources ("a notorious front for Chinese espionage," according to the *New York Times*'s William Safire) to the White House to meet with Gore's chief of staff Jack Quinn and possibly with Gore himself.

When the Senate Government Affairs Committee tried to question her, Hsia invoked the Fifth Amendment. The Committee report concluded that Hsia "may ultimately have funneled $146,400 to various U.S. political candidates. Of this total, $116,500 went to the DNC in support of the Clinton/Gore ticket."

▲

Rather than a more or less accidental slipup, the Buddhist Temple incident was an example of Clinton/Gore's new approach to fundraising. In 1995, presidential pollster Dick Morris had warned Clinton that he might not be re-elected in 1996, and suggested an early media campaign to turn the polls around. Team Clinton tore down the walls mandated by election law between the Clinton/Gore campaign and the Democratic National Committee. Despite a pledge signed by both men only to spend "hard money" which their campaign raised in accordance with set limits, Clinton, Gore and their aides raised unlimited "soft money" contributions for the DNC and directed exactly how the money would be spent. As Bob Woodward wrote, Clinton himself picked out the photograph of himself that was to appear in a DNC ad—which showed that the president had abandoned even the pretense of spending limits. Gore later would admit to the FBI that both he and Clinton reviewed DNC ads before they ran.

The DNC held what would be called "donor maintenance events" inside the White House, selling access to the president, vice president and first lady. Terry McAuliffe, the Clinton crony who later helped Hillary buy a house in New York and now works as a Gore fundraiser, proposed offering big donors and money raisers "overnights" in the Lincoln bedroom. The White House held 103 coffees for its boosters and big donors. White House aide Harold Ickes made their purpose explicit by calling them "political/fundraising coffees." Ickes sent biweekly reports to the president and vice president detailing how much these events brought in.

DNC deputy chief of staff Martha Phipps wrote a memo in which she suggested selling off seats on Air Force One and Air Force Two, permission to play on White House tennis courts, participation in official delegations traveling abroad, visits to and overnight stays in the White House, "photo opportunities with the President, Vice President, First Lady and Mrs. Gore," "phone time with the Vice President," lunches with the First Lady, Mack McLarty or Ira Magaziner, and "meetings with Vice President Gore."

Big donor Johnny Chung delivered the most famous—and

apt—description of the Clinton White House when he told the *Los Angeles Times*, "The White House is like a subway: You have to put in coins to open the gates." And open the gates he did. Chung contributed $366,000 to the Democratic National Committee in exchange for being able to use the White House as a place to entertain clients. National Security Council aide Robert Suettinger had warned White House aides that Chung was a "hustler" who "should be treated with a pinch of suspicion." Still, Chung visited the White House some fifty times.

Gore regularly sat in on White House weekly strategy meetings to discuss how to spend party money. (He observed at one session that the Democratic National Committee could raise the money it needed "only if the President and I actually do the events, the calls, the coffees, etc.") Gore later insisted that "there was a clear distinction" between the DNC and the Clinton/Gore campaign. "There was a separate message. There were separate legal requirements; it was separate in almost all respects." But even Democrats on the Thompson committee rejected that notion in their minority report: "Tens of millions of soft dollars are raised by the parties and spent, through such devices as 'issue advocacy' ads, for the benefit of candidates."

The White House spin, which Gore would endorse, held that the problem wasn't that people in the Clinton White House broke the law, but rather that the laws allowed them to do such things. Yet Common Cause asked Attorney General Janet Reno to appoint a special counsel to look into possible criminal misconduct on the part of the Clinton and Dole campaigns and the Democratic and Republican National Committees. Thompson Committee lead counsel Michael Madigan later explained, "It should have been looked at. It was done to an extent never previously done. What the outcome would have been, I don't know. The lines are not clear in the law."

Like Gore, Chung also blamed the system for allowing him

to do what he did. But if the system *had* permitted him to do what he did, he would not have been forced to accept a plea bargain that sentenced him to five years' probation for tax evasion and bank fraud. Judge Manuel Real, who sentenced Chung, did not buy the party line and said he had trouble believing that Don Fowler and Richard Sullivan, now a Gore money man, didn't know what was going on.

Gore's old pal John Huang also got a sweet deal with the Reno Department of Justice. The DNC was forced to return some $1.6 million of the $3.4 million he had raised. Huang reportedly later told the FBI that his former employer James Riady had approved an illegal scheme to launder $700,000 to the DNC, but Huang was never charged with laundering contributions. Instead, he pleaded guilty to one felony charge for making an illegal $2,500 contribution to the campaign of Los Angeles mayoral candidate Mike Woo in 1993 and an illegal $5,000 contribution to a Victory Fund that benefited the campaign of Senator Dianne Feinstein in 1994. While the felony charge could have landed Huang behind bars for five long years, the Department of Justice announced it would not seek a prison term, and the *Los Angeles Times* reported that prosecutors even agreed to write a letter supporting the restoration of the civic-minded Huang's voting rights.

The FBI questioned Gore some four times before April 2000, yet not once did they ask him about John Huang, Maria Hsia or the temple fundraiser. It seemed that the Department of Justice had a policy of Don't Ask/Don't Know.

The Phone Prince

Like some literary concept of original sin spreading outward to contaminate everything about it, the Clinton scandals began to engulf Gore despite his attempts to paint himself as a Boy Scout trapped in a bordello. In March 1997, the *Washington Post* ran an article by Bob Woodward reporting that the supposedly upright Gore had become known "at the DNC as the administration's 'solicitor-in-chief.'" The term enraged the vice president. Later, when the FBI questioned Gore about phone calls he had made, as mentioned in the story, he told agents that six months before the piece ran, Woodward had asked him for his help in writing about the election. When Gore refused, he told the FBI, according to a Bureau report, that he feared that Woodward would "come after me." Gore added that he actually was relieved when the article finally came out because that meant Woodward had spent all that time on the piece, and couldn't come up with anything particularly damning.

For a story with no substance, it certainly caused a stir. Woodward had reported that the vice president, unlike his predecessors, was ready, willing and able to call up corporate executives and ask them for campaign money. The story reported how Gore called James L. Donald, a Republican and chairman of DSC Communications, a telecommunications firm, to thank him for a $100,000 corporate contribution to the DNC that was "intended, in part, as a reward to the administration for Commerce Department assistance" in winning a $36 million contract in Mexico. Gore told one person he called, "I've been tasked with raising $2 million by the end of the week and you're on my list." One Gore friend who got such a call told Woodward, "It's revolting." Another complained, "There were elements of a shakedown in the call. It was very awkward. For a vice president, particularly this vice president who has real power and is the heir apparent, to ask for money gave me no choice. I have so much business that touches on the federal government—the telecommunications act, tax policy, regulations galore." The shakedown worked. The friend immediately sent a check for $100,000 to the DNC.

The newspaper story which Gore tried to dismiss also led

to what must be deemed the most disastrous press conference of his career. Later, it would be learned that aides had warned Gore that he wasn't ready to address the public, but his daughter Karenna had urged him to meet with the press to kill the story. That's not how events worked out, largely because Gore used the term "no controlling legal authority" seven times in twenty-four minutes. As in: "There is no controlling legal authority that says any of these activities violated any law." This was something of a ruse: "No controlling legal authority" is legalese for the assertion that, since no one had ever been successfully convicted for violating this law before, no one was quite sure how the law worked. Moreover, rather than voicing remorse for his ethically suspect behavior, Gore asserted that actually he was "very proud" of his fundraising prowess. He insisted, "I never did anything I thought was wrong." And: "I understood what I did to be legal and appropriate. I felt like I was doing the right thing." Then, his pride in his fundraising prowess notwithstanding, Gore vowed never to dial for dollars from the White House ever again.

Gore told reporters that other vice presidents had done the same as he did, although Walter Mondale, George Bush and Dan Quayle all denied soliciting campaign funds as vice presidents. And it was more than a technical violation of protocol. It is one thing to appear at a fundraising dinner where everyone is present by choice, but quite another for a sitting vice president or president personally to call a corporate CEO asking for donations, thereby making it very difficult for the executive to say no. Gore never acknowledged stepping over an ethical bright line. In explaining that he would not make phone calls from the White House again, he also tried to reassert his lost innocence: "If I had realized in advance that this would cause such concern, then I wouldn't have done it in the first place." The shrewd Marjorie Williams wrote later in the *Washington Post*, "The most startling fact I learned was that Gore never really stopped and considered, on the merits, whether a sitting vice president who made calls to CEOs asking for contributions in specific amounts might seem to be running something of a shakedown."

A byproduct of the Woodward piece was the later discovery that Gore not only made fundraising calls, but also made them from the White House. Was that legal? The 1883 Pendleton Act stated that it is "unlawful for any person to solicit or receive any contributions" in a federal workplace. An April 1995 memo written by then–White House counsel Abner Mikva warned that "Campaign activities of any kind are prohibited in or from Government buildings. This means fundraising events may not be held in the White House; also, no fundraising phone calls or mail may emanate from the White House."

Gore said there was no problem because "all of the calls that I made were charged to the DNC"—which turned out to be untrue. (He used a Clinton/Gore '96 credit card for some of the calls, which meant he used the credit card of a campaign that can't accept more than $1,000 per individual to raise $100,000 contributions.) When reporters asked Gore about the Mikva memo, he responded that he thought the memo was "addressed to White House employees other than the president and vice president." He admitted he made calls from his office on a "few occasions." Gore later told the FBI he made forty-six to fifty phone solicitations. (Bill Turque put the number at seventy-one.) The Thompson Committee estimated that the calls made on these few occasions raised as much as $800,000 for the DNC.

The argument could be made that his years in the Clinton White House had changed Gore. As a senator, he had respected the letter of the law, leaving his office if he needed to make fundraising calls (although he felt it was kosher to leave his congressional office phone number for return calls). In 1994, when

Gore, now vice president, made calls for the DNC that raised some $400,000 for congressional campaigns, he used telephones outside the White House.

Then something happened. This is how the FBI described Gore's change in phone call venues after interviewing him in November 1997: "Vice President Gore stated that he assumed that the DNC fundraising calls were going to be handled in the same manner [initiated and dialed from former Gore aide Peter Knight's office]. However, at some point during the initial DNC fundraising calls, Vice President Gore became aware that the calls were being initiated and dialed from his office. Vice President Gore advised that he realized there was a departure from this earlier practice and then asked his Executive Assistant, 'is it alright?' He stated that his Executive Assistant replied, 'yes, we have a credit card.'"

At first, Attorney General Janet Reno determined there was no need for an independent counsel because Gore raised "soft money" for the DNC. Then the *Washington Post* revealed that Gore had raised hard money as well. (Half of the money the DNC spends must come from individual donations under $20,000— that's the party's "hard money.") Reno was forced to appoint an independent counsel to investigate whether Gore lied to federal investigators about the hard money.

Aides insisted that Gore did not realize he was raising hard money for the DNC, which is certainly plausible. But a series of memos written by Harold Ickes pointed out the need to raise such hard money so that more soft money could be spent. In June 1996, for example, Ickes wrote, "It does little good to raise large amounts [of corporate contributions over $20,000] if the amount of the [individual donations under $20,000] are insufficient to permit the spending of the former." In an August memo, Ickes quipped that it is called hard money "because it's hard to raise." Gore told the FBI that he did not read the memos because

203

(adding a dig at Ickes and Morris) they were "ideological tracts" from the "struggle" between the two men.

Gore also told the FBI that a November 21, 1995, meeting would not have included a discussion about the number of phone calls that had to be made. Later a copy of a memo surfaced that proved Gore's version of events to be untrue. Gore aide David Strauss had taken down the vice president's remarks at the November meeting. He circled an item calling for "10 calls by VPOTUS" (Vice President of the United States). He wrote that Gore said, "Count me in on the calls," and also volunteered, "Is it possible to do a reallocation for me to take more of the events and the calls?" (Which shows there is some truth in the jokes that Gore is like the student who raises his hand to remind the teacher she forgot to assign homework.) After the memo surfaced, Gore's memory got shaky. He told the FBI that he drank a lot of iced tea at the meetings, which necessitated many trips to the men's room, so he might have missed all this talk about phone calls. When the FBI asked Gore about Strauss's notes, according to the FBI report, "Vice President Gore would not dispute that what is reflected in the notes was said at the meeting. Vice President Gore simply did not hear those things said."

But how could Gore not have heard those things said when he is the person who said them?

In November 1998 the ever-compliant Janet Reno determined that there was no need for an investigation: "I can see no reasonable basis for concluding that he had a motive to tell this story if it were not true."

The Greatest President

On the day the House voted to impeach Bill Clinton for lying under oath before a grand jury, Al Gore acted as the head cheerleader in what later became known as the White House pep rally. In the preceding weeks there had been talk of Clinton stepping down and letting Gore replace him, but while the vice president was always the first to scotch such talk, the Gore family's semiotics made it clear that they were not wholly supportive of Bill Clinton. Tipper Gore did not show up at the White House rally. (She later told the *New York Times* she didn't remember what she was doing at the time.) But Al Gore was once again the dutiful son. He stood in front of an angry legion of House members and told the world that Bill Clinton would be considered "one of our greatest presidents."

When Gore started his own run for the presidency, he tried to distance himself from that heady moment. On CBS's *Face the Nation,* he said of his friend, "The Republican Senate was about to try to remove him from office for an offense which, while terrible, was in the judgment of the American people not one that justified removal from office. We were in the midst of political combat and I think that fighting back to try to prevent a political injustice from occurring justifies drawing the line in the sand and saying hold on here, look at the great achievements that we have."

Still, candidate Gore would tell the American people that he was a champion for good government. His strategy was previewed by former White House fundraising scandal spokesman Lanny Davis in his book *Truth to Tell: Notes from My White House Education*. Davis explained the "key" to the administration's approach: "During the Watergate era, the Nixon people tried to say that 'everybody does it,' and that makes it okay. What we were saying was, 'Everybody does it and it's not okay. So let's clean up the system.' That's why in our daily strategy sessions, during and after the White House coffees story, we would always add: We've got to clean the system up, both parties, through comprehensive campaign finance reform."

It was a rhetorical magic act, the electoral equivalent of Stop Me Before I Kill Again. By saying they didn't believe that what they did should have been legal and the system had to be changed, Clinton and Gore inoculated themselves. Thus Gore felt free to brag that the administration's record on ethics was the "highest in the history of the White House." The solicitor-in-chief who had told reporters he was "very proud" of his fundraising prowess boasted in his first primary debate with Bill Bradley, "I promise you I will fight my heart out to get meaningful campaign finance reform and get the influence of big money out of the political system." Transparent as it was, the strategy worked. No one asked Gore after he made that pledge, "What happened in 1996? Had your heart stopped working then?"

As the 2000 campaign moved into high gear, Gore began to campaign as the candidate who would be better on campaign finance reform, even as he surrounded himself with some of the more ethically challenged names in Democratic politics.

For instance, Tony Coelho, his campaign chairman, is a former member of the House who resigned in 1989 just in time to scuttle a House Ethics Committee investigation into a sweetheart $100,000 junk-bond deal he had failed to disclose, and who was the subject of Brooks Jackson's book *Honest Graft*. Months after Coelho took hold of the campaign reins, he found himself embroiled in a new scandal. The Center for Public Integrity disclosed that the inspector general had looked into Coelho's tenure as the commissioner general of the U.S. pavilion at the 1998 World Exposition in Portugal. Just as Coelho received no salary from Gore, he was not paid for the Portugal post, either. Still, Coelho spent his time in an $18,000-per-month apartment in Portugal, paid for by taxpayers. While Expo '98 had a fleet of six vans "which were underutilized," Coelho spent $800 for a chauffeur-driven Mercedes, an expense the inspector general considered "especially troublesome." Coelho's young niece Debra also happened to get a job with the Expo, for which she was paid $2,500 per month.

Having had so much practice looking the other way in the Clinton White House, Gore knew exactly how to react. He said this about Coelho on CBS's *Face the Nation:* "I haven't seen this report, but I know him, and he is going to continue doing the terrific job he's been doing as my campaign chair." He later told the *New York Times* that if Coelho managed the campaign well, "the smudges of the past would take care of themselves."

But the smudges became darker. Months later the *National Journal* reported that the independent counsel's audit had resulted in a criminal referral to the Department of Justice. The story reported that Coelho may have used Expo '98 to woo investors in an effort to raise $6 million for an Internet startup company, LoanNet, by putting two stepsons of one investor (who happened to be the U.S. ambassador to Portugal) on the payroll and flying two potential investors to Portugal with Expo '98 plane tickets so they could stay in the $18,000-a-month luxury digs. Coelho's attorney Stanley Brand denied any criminal wrongdoing on his client's part. But the *National Journal* discovered that Coelho had arranged for Brand to get a $60,000-a-year part-time job as counsel to the Democratic members on the U.S. Census Monitoring Board and that Brand had hired a private investigator to dig up dirt on a federal employee cooperating with the investigation of Coelho.

Former Clinton/Gore chairman Pete Knight is also part of the Gore inner circle. In 1997 the Justice Department investigated Knight after it was learned that one of his clients, Molten Metal Technology, had won $32 million in federal energy contracts for a toxic waste disposal method that failed to deliver as promised. The Department filed no charges against Knight.

Terry McAuliffe, the man behind the White House's creative ways of "servicing" donors by such innovations as renting out the

Lincoln bedroom, is a big Gore fundraiser. The Justice Department investigated what it deemed to be an illegal $375,000 consulting fee arrangement between McAuliffe and the Prudential Insurance Company. The Department charged Prudential, not McAuliffe. He also has been implicated in an alleged money-laundering scheme between the Teamsters and the DNC, which led a federal jury in New York to convict union boss William H. Hamilton for diverting $885,000 in union funds to Democratic political organizations and sentence him to three years.

Richard Sullivan, the man who told John Huang he didn't raise enough money at the Hsi Lai Temple event, is also on the Gore payroll. Sullivan reportedly has worked out some sort of cooperation agreement with the Justice Department on the Teamster money-laundering case. Sullivan's testimony has conflicted with McAuliffe's, but that's the sort of detail Gore is adept at overlooking.

Little Fish Goes Up the River

As Gore was trying to put all this tawdry activity behind him and reinvent himself as a champion of campaign reform, there was still the unfinished business of Maria Hsia.

When her case went to trial, it appeared that a not-guilty verdict was inevitable. The Department of Justice never seemed particularly interested in getting to the bottom of what happened at the Hsi Lai Temple. Former Thompson Committee counsel Michael Madigan bitterly noted,

> *The Justice Department did not pursue John Huang the way a normal prosecutor would, did not indict when they should have indicted him back in 1997 when the Thompson Committee introduced evidence (that he did illegal stuff), did not indict him on the Buddhist*

208

Temple event although he clearly was involved with the laundering of money there—and two years later gave him a slap on the wrist. No one will ever know everything that Huang knows because of the bungled prosecution.

The Department did indict Hsia for causing false statements to be filed with federal election officials in cases related to her infamous money laundering at the Buddhist Temple, as well as illegal contributions she raised for Representative Patrick Kennedy (D-R.I.). But everything seemed to be going in her favor.

The prosecutor, Eric Yaffe, also had been the prosecutor in the case of Franklin L. Haney, a long-time Gore supporter and the only other person brought to trial for the 1996 money-laundering scandals. A jury acquitted Haney, yet the Justice Department kept Jaffe on the Hsia prosecution, although he had a losing record for what observers believed was an easier case. Judge Paul L. Friedman, a Clinton appointee, was selected to oversee the case against Hsia instead of a judge who had been chosen by the normal method of pool selection. Two years before, Friedman had dismissed these very charges against Hsia because of what he called the Justice Department's "Alice in Wonderland" logic in accusing Hsia of causing false statements to be made, not of violating election law by her money laundering. (An appellate court disagreed with Friedman's logic and sent the case back to him.)

Two Buddhist nuns subpoenaed to testify against Hsia skipped the country before the trial. As the *Memphis Commercial Appeal* reported, the attorney for the Venerable Man Ho told a federal judge that traveling to the U.S. for the trial would "negatively impact her religious duties." Friedman refused to allow the nuns' testimony to be admitted as evidence, which made prosecutor Yaffe's job that much harder.

Trial watchers expected the jury to acquit, but after ten

hours of deliberation, it found Hsia guilty of all five counts against her. Said Gore, "The jury has rendered a verdict. It's a hard day for her. She's been a friend and a political supporter. But since this matter is still in the courts, I won't comment on it." It was March 2000. Twenty-two people had been charged in the 1996 fundraising scandals, sixteen had pleaded guilty, and for the first time, to the great surprise of trial watchers, a jury had found someone guilty. Said Senator Fred Thompson, "I don't know who is more surprised, me or the Justice Department."

CHAPTER TEN

The New New Al Gore

The 2000 campaign started off like a bad joke. Al Gore made so many gaffes that the Republican National Committee felt it could make him into a national laughing-stock just as the Democrats had Dan Quayle a few years earlier. Throughout the summer of 1999 it seemed that every day brought a new e-mail from the RNC with some new comical statement or action by the vice president. There was the Gore claim that he had taken "the initiative in creating the Internet," which helped recycle his earlier off-the-wall assertion that Tipper and he were inspirations for the lead characters of *Love Story,* and all the other fables that seemed to mark him, if not as a pathological liar, at least as a man of such uncertain ego that he needed to pad his already impressive resume with preposterously false claims.

It seemed doubtful that so fatuous a figure as he had come to appear could win over the voters. In September, when New York Senator Daniel Patrick Moynihan endorsed Bill Bradley, his aides assured reporters that Moynihan had a great deal of respect for Gore. Still, the venerable politician's explanation for his pick must have felt like a kick in the stomach to the vice president: "Nothing is the matter with Mr. Gore except he can't be elected president."

Gore's image also suffered after he tried to distance himself from Bill Clinton. After years of playing up his loyalty, Gore appeared on network television—on the day he announced his candidacy for the White House—denouncing Clinton's behavior as "inexcusable." Just as Gore mistakenly had seen his father as a liability, not an asset, when he first ran for Congress in 1976, the vice president now saw his boss as a drag—to the anger of many Democrats. It didn't help. Gore's attempts to distance himself, less than seven months after the White House pep rally, made him appear as a craven opportunist, willing to be on whatever side of Clinton that got him the most votes. Meanwhile, newspapers were filled with accounts of a rift between Clinton and Gore, especially after the president called the *New York Times* in May to assert his faith in Gore's ultimate victory, but nonetheless undercutting that statement by telling Richard L. Berke he thought Gore should loosen up and "have a good time."

An event Gore's consultants put together in July 1999 showed what a difficult time Team Gore was having getting things right. With taxpayers footing the bill, Gore traveled to New Hampshire to announce a grant of $819,000 for river projects, including $100,000 for the Connecticut River Joint Commission. It was supposed to be a moment when Gore showed how the administration, with him as environmental point man, had helped clean up the nation's rivers. It was also an outdoor photo op, where Gore could dump the suit and tie that had become a metaphor for his notorious stiffness.

With New Hampshire Governor Jeanne Sheehan, Gore piled into a canoe as television cameras and print photographers captured the moment they launched into the Connecticut River. There was only one problem: the river was too shallow for a canoe that morning. So, the officials sent out the call to Pacific Gas and Electric, and the utility company immediately released a mega-gush of water—half a billion gallons—to raise the water level by eight to ten inches. The outing immediately turned into a lose-lose situation as one local official griped to Bill Sammon of the *Washington Times*, "They won't release water for the fish when we ask them to, but somehow they find themselves able to release it for a politician." The Republican National Committee had another windfall, as one state GOP official filed a complaint with the Federal Election Commission calling the water an in-kind contribution from the utility. Gore 2000 and New Hampshire Democrats give conflicting accounts—trying to shift the blame and any knowledge away from the Gore camp—which made a one-day story play out for days.

Once again, Al Gore looked like a buffoon. The champion of the low-flush toilet had been caught riding on millions of gallons of water that could have been conserved for human needs. Once again, Gore was portrayed as the opportunist who would stick his face anywhere if a camera was nearby.

In the summer of 1999, the hugely expensive Gore campaign looked like the gang that couldn't spit straight. Yet within six months, Gore's operation would be a lean, mean hit machine. And Gore would be sporting the mantle of invincibility.

▲

The transition was not smooth. Reflecting the vice president's own weakness for psychobabble, the Gore campaign had a puzzling tendency to maunder over its every move and to explain its rationale for every decision. Gore had graduated from being the vice president who wanted cabinet secretaries to be in touch with their childhood years, to the would-be president who wanted to share all his thoughts and feelings on the campaign with anyone who would listen. It made every move the campaign adopted seem transparent, part of some gimmick to lure voters.

Every decision entailed an analysis. When the campaign decided that Gore no longer would speak behind a lectern in his appearances but instead would move around on stage with a hand mike Oprah-style, the staff made sure the press understood this was a deliberate move. Aides even told reporters they had commanded Gore not to tell any more jokes about his wooden-ness, which had been part of his standard stump shtick for years. As the primary season began and Gore challenged Bill Bradley to dispense with 30-second ads and debate on a regular basis, Gore consultant Bob Shrum told the media that he suggested the idea.

That these announcements made Gore seem even more manufactured, more like a robo-candidate assembled by com-mittee, did not seem to dawn on Team Gore. Nor did the fact that all these well-choreographed transitions would make the candidate, as well as his campaign, seem opportunistic. Indeed, in February 2000 a *New York Times*/CBS News poll found that 61 percent of Americans polled thought Gore would tell people what he thought they wanted to hear—compared to 38 percent who thought the same of primary opponent Bill Bradley.

Gore managed to turn his campaign around by moving it. On September 29, 1999, he announced that he was moving Gore 2000 "lock, stock and barrel" from Washington to Nashville. His aides told the press—once again—to be prepared for "a new Al Gore" who would frame his campaign from his old home, Ten-nessee, not from inside the Beltway. The New Al Gore would be his own man, not the creature of his platoon of pollsters, as the soul of his campaign moved from K Street to Kmart. Campaign spokesman Chris Lehane told reporters that the candidate wanted to spend more time with "real" people.

It was hard news for campaign staff, who at this point numbered more than 110 employees, with 19 of them earning more than $50,000 a year. The campaign put out the word that anyone who wanted to go to Nashville was welcome to stay on, although behind the scenes, the top tier of advisers let certain aides know their services were not needed. Gore told reporters, "What I told the staff this morning was that I am more grateful than I can express in words for the hard work that each and every man and woman here has put into this campaign. And for those who make this journey to Nashville with us, it's going to be fun."

Team Gore timed the announcement of this New Al Gore to preempt more bad news. As newspapers were soon to report, Democratic rival Bill Bradley had raised about $6.7 million between July and September—more than Gore's $6.5 million. Gore would have less cash on hand than Bradley, since Gore had spent $6 million during that quarter, compared to Bradley's $4.2 million. It was a low point.

Initially, the press and the Republican National Committee gleefully ridiculed the retreat to Nashville as another desperate gimmick by a campaign careening off course. The RNC bought a billboard outside of Gore's Nashville headquarters with a photo of Gore and Clinton in a bear hug. Pundits guffawed at the notion of someone like Al Gore, born and bred in the Beltway, calling Nashville his home. Others compared the move to Bob Dole's desperate decision in 1996 to quit the Senate in order to boost his doomed campaign.

But Gore stuck to his New Al Gore strategy despite the cynical reception. He knew, if all the Gore-watchers didn't, that what was new had more to do with psychology than with geography. It was not the soil of Tennessee that Gore was returning to, but his attack-dog roots.

Within a few weeks, the press corps was no longer making fun of Gore but pitying Bill Bradley as a man who didn't know what hit him. Bradley had hoped to conduct a different kind of campaign, more decorous and professorial, less filled with the rancor and mudslinging of recent races. But once Bradley started getting traction in the polls, Gore plowed into him like a runaway train, shamelessly and at times viciously seizing on anything to destroy his candidacy. Gore hit Bradley for suggesting "programs without price tags," even though Gore himself had avoided telling what many of the programs he proposed would cost. Gore hit Bradley for being a quitter—because he had retired from the Senate. If Gore was an "underdog," as he claimed, it was primarily because he, more than any other contemporary politician, knew how and where to bite. His attack team was so strong that during the Gore-Bradley debates, it handed journalists page-long rebuttals of Bradley's statements while the debate was still going on.

Some campaign pranks were downright funny. After a debate in which Bradley suggested that people should lead more healthy lives to keep medical costs down, seniors in sweat suits showed up in front of Bradley's Iowa headquarters and did jumping jacks. Other highjinks were less kind. Overzealous Gore supporters in New Hampshire screamed at a Democratic congressman who supported Bradley, and purposefully splattered mud on Senator Bob Kerrey, reportedly making crude remarks about the disabilities the war hero had suffered in Vietnam. When asked about this behavior, Gore spokesman Chris Lehane defended the First Amendment rights of the "demonstrators."

Riding his Disconnect, Gore, of course, styled himself as the clean campaigner. "Personal attacks have no place in a campaign," he chided Bradley in November. "Sometimes Bill gets a little out of sorts when I talk about the substance of policy," Gore told the *Washington Post* as the contest heated up, adding the jaw-dropping comment, "I certainly do not want to talk about him as a person, especially not in a critical way."

In December, when Bradley refused to say that he would not

raise taxes to pay for his health plan, Gore jumped at the chance to mischaracterize his opponent's position: "To propose a possible tax increase, not because of some contingency related to unknowns in the economy but because of an inability to cover a huge gaping hole in a campaign promise that can't be covered in any other way—that is irresponsible." And: "I'm talking about tax cuts, Senator Bradley is talking about tax increases." (Gore had said in a different context that he wouldn't make a no-new-taxes pledge either.) He attacked Bradley for receiving too much campaign money from pharmaceutical companies, even though two of his own closest advisers, Tom Downey and Pete Knight, were paid lobbyists for the industry.

Then, having savaged his opponent so brutally, Gore piously told him, "I will never run a personal negative ad against you." Frustrated Bradley aides sent out a flyer on the disease of "Gore-itis," whose chief symptom was "uncontrollable lying." Bradley quickly apologized for his aides' highjinks. A theatrically downcast Gore sadly remarked, "It's especially disappointing coming from a candidate who promised not to do that sort of thing." Gore then used Bradley's apology against him, charging in a January 2000 debate, "Senator Bradley is the only one who has been forced by the media to apologize for negative attacks in this campaign."

And it worked. Gore's gimmicks—especially the New Al Gore's desire to get to know every voter in New Hampshire—seemed so transparent, so phony, that Bradley supporters believed voters would see through them. The *San Francisco Chronicle*'s Marc Sandalow reported that after the New Al Gore asked a female questioner during a political debate, "How is your son doing?" many of those present "rolled their eyes." But while voters may have groaned, they also pulled the lever for the vice president. When he knocked Bradley out in the debates, leaving him barely able to fight back, Gore's strong performance robbed Bradley supporters of the reason many said they supported him. By fighting so hard, Gore demonstrated that he, not the stoical Bradley, had the killer instinct.

As soon as he had won enough delegates to claim the nomination, Gore immediately stepped up his attacks on George W. Bush. He questioned whether Bush had the experience to be president. His aides frequently cited the forty-fifth placement of Texas SAT-takers in the country. He also hit the Bush record on the environment.

The most breathtaking punch in Gore's attack, however, came in the spring of 2000 when he decided to claim the mantle of campaign reformer. In a March interview with the *New York Times,* Gore explained that he planned to differentiate himself from Bush by showing America that he was the real reformer. America's paper of record clearly did not know how to react to such brass. A March 12 headline read, "Gore to Embrace Campaign Finance as Central Theme," with a subhead, "Acts on a Vulnerability."

The tactic spoke volumes about the candidate. Any other politician who had been ridiculed as solicitor-in-chief of a tawdry administration, had corrupted religious institutions by conniving at money-laundering contribution schemes, and had shaken down donors from the White House would have regarded campaign finance reform as his scarlet letter. Not Gore. His Disconnect had always worked for him; it would work for him again. All he had to do was keep repeating that he had strong convictions on this issue. He hadn't walked the walk, but he could talk the talk endlessly. He could attack George W. Bush for his fundraising crimes. He would admit that he himself was an "imperfect messenger," but he alone had the moral courage to get the message of campaign reform out from under the shadow cast by the Republican Party. He would keep repeating this mantra and soon his guilty past would fall away from him like the spent booster of a rocket that continued its upward course.

When *New York Times* reporters asked Gore about his record, he remained firm in his claim that he would fight for cleaner politics. No controlling legal authority? "That's old news," he replied. News accounts that former White House chief of staff Leon Panetta said he was listening intently when aides discussed raising hard money for the DNC with the vice president? "I don't know what is in that particular paper and I can't comment on something that hasn't been publicly released that I haven't seen," Gore responded insouciantly. What about calls for a new investigation in light of this new information? The way the *Times* handled Gore's response to this question says it all: "[Laughs.] That was all reviewed three years ago."

Most important of all—and straight from Clinton's Monica Lewinsky playbook—the vice president noted, "I have acknowledged my mistakes. I have learned from my mistakes." He had never actually admitted doing anything wrong when caught in the fundraising scandals, yet now he said he had learned from his mistakes. In that logical gap was Gore's true genius as a politician.

In his passage from Prince of Goredom to the man who stood ready to sit on the throne his parents had groomed him for, Gore had learned the secret of perfect obfuscation: There is no past. In these modern times of tabloidized revelation, when everyone is in recovery from something, the audacious man can not only walk away from what he has done, but from what he has been. And he can frame this transformation in such a way as to make those who insist upon the truth seem merely petty.

▲

Just before Super Tuesday, as Gore was telling reporters that he was not going to take a single vote for granted, he already knew that he had won the nomination. He wouldn't admit it, but you could see it in the way he had begun subtly to change his positions, no longer worried that Bradley would outflank him on the left. During a debate with his demoralized opponent in Harlem, for instance, Gore suddenly switched from earnestly explaining the need for affirmative action to voicing his horror at quotas. In an appearance before the *San Francisco Chronicle* editorial board, Gore, who had been excoriating Bradley on abortion, now mentioned that while he was of course steadfast in supporting a woman's right to choose, he was personally opposed to abortion.

It was in an interview with *Rolling Stone* that Gore detoured most sharply from a position he had taken when Bill Bradley was still a factor in the campaign. While the media had pasted Governor Bush for supporting tough drug laws while supposedly having had a checkered chemical past of his own, Gore had enjoyed a free ride on drugs. (Even Bill Turque's revelation that the vice president's former friend John Warneke claimed to have smoked pot with Gore for years sank like a stone.) But the vice president knew that his interviewers from *Rolling Stone* would ask him about his positions on drugs and drug laws, and he was prepared for a Sister Souljah moment.

Asked if he supported mandatory minimum sentences for drug convictions, Gore answered, "I have supported them. I think that drawing a hard line against marijuana use is the right thing to do. I know we disagree on that."

Earlier in the primaries, when it was still necessary to appear liberal, the vice president had come out guardedly in favor of medical marijuana at a town hall meeting in New Hampshire. As the *Washington Post* reported, Gore told the audience that doctors "ought to have the option" of using marijuana "to alleviate pain." In explaining his position, Gore once again mentioned his sister Nancy Hunger Gore, for whom marijuana was prescribed during treatment for lung cancer. "[She] decided against it because she didn't like it; it didn't produce the desired result," he explained. "If it had worked for her, I think she should have had the ability to get her pain relieved that way." Gore acknowledged that his position ran counter to that of drug czar Barry McCaffrey.

Later, however, with the nomination in the bag, Gore's tone on the issue changed. In the interview with *Rolling Stone,* he said, "The issue ought to be decided on the basis of science and not on the basis of a political judgment." And he said that he would support legalizing medical marijuana only if research showed it has "uniquely beneficial medical properties." He added, "And pending that, I am not in favor of the medical use." And then he used the memory of Nancy Gore one more time: "My sister was prescribed marijuana cigarettes when she was going through chemotherapy in an effort to save her life from lung cancer, and that was during a time when Tennessee had legalized medicinal marijuana."

"Did she use it?" *Rolling Stone* asked.

"Yes, and it did not work for her. Thus far, the research does not justify its use. And so I oppose it."

And so the story comes full circle. Al Gore saying whatever he thinks he has to say to win. Al Gore using his sister's death to justify a position. Al Gore flip-flopping and using his family as a buffer for his position. Al Gore defying and denying his past.

From tobakka to weed: in Goredom, the more things change, the more they stay the same.

ACKNOWLEDGMENTS

Many of my friends who have written books have confided to me that they were shocked at how little input they received from their editor. My own experience with my editor, Peter Collier, was completely different. I'm sure he had no idea what a challenge he had invited upon himself when he signed me up for this book, but he met it willingly and worked hard for me. I found the switch from column-writing to book-writing a difficult one; and to the extent that this book flows, Peter Collier deserves the credit.

My research assistant, Jennifer Nelson, did yeoman work as she balanced research with graduate studies in journalism and motherhood. I also owe thanks to research pinch-hitter Sheri Annis, to copy editor Carol Staswick, to Trisha Lisk, and to Judy Hardin, who kept everything on track.

Undoubtedly the person who has suffered the most through the writing of this book is my husband, Wesley J. Smith. There is not an insult hurled by a woman in labor that my husband hasn't heard from me in this last year. Yet my admiration for him has grown as I consider that he managed to write nine books with far more grace than I. My family deserves thanks for listening to my constant grousing, so thanks to Jim, Vickie, Stephen, Leslie, Jennifer, Jeremiah, Rebecca, Eric and Joshua Saunders, as well as my amazing mother-in-law, Leona Smith. who always managed to sound completely fascinated with the dirty details of my workload. Special thanks go to Chloe Barrett, my feline collaborator, who often napped happily next to me as I slaved on.

I must acknowledge the support and forbearance of the *San Francisco Chronicle,* most especially editorial page editor John Diaz, and managing editor Jerry Roberts. *Chronicle* readers often voice their amazement that the paper allows me to express my usually conservative views. I in turn remind them that the *Chronicle* not only allows me to express those opinions, but also pays me for the pleasure.

My pals Allison Hayward, Steve Hayward, Carolyn Lochhead, Tom Meyer, and Peter B. Collins kindly reviewed all or parts of the book and gave welcome and sage advice. I thank them for their input and for their understanding where I have failed to incorporate all of their wisdom. I'm sure that I have forgotten some friends who had ideas that panned out, served as willing sounding boards or otherwise contributed to this book, but I do have the presence of mind to thank information goddess Julia House, Janice Greene, Carla Marinucci, Marc Sandalow, Kathleen Rhodes, Joe Rodota, Scott Lindlaw, Dan Kramer, Lois Riley, Jonathan Tolman, and Mike McKeown.

Through his office, Vice President Gore turned down my request for an interview. In the course of writing my column for the *Chronicle,* however, I have called his campaign and White House office and found that his staffers live up to their reputation for diligently returning phone calls, even from known critics. Press secretary Chris Lehane in particular earns his pay. Many of the quotes attributed to Gore in this book come from prepared remarks that were posted on his White House or campaign Web sites. Thus, the words I quote may not be the exact words that Gore uttered, but they are the very words that his staff chose to leave for posterity.

Even as I finished this book, I felt that my work was undone by the fact that the vice president's proposals, like some of his ideas, have a tendency to change. It is also true that the Gore 2000 tab continues to grow. In May 2000, for example, the vice president announced, "Let's give every teacher a $5,000 raise." I suggest that readers consider what I have written to be Gore's minimum campaign proposals, and expect that they will become more grandiose, especially if he continues to trail in the national polls.

Rather than use footnotes, I have chosen to credit sources as they are cited. While I have been critical of many aspects of Gore reportage, the journalists named in this book have written excellent, substantive reports that are a credit to the trade. I thank the gods daily that I work in a field that is so challenging, interesting and downright fun. And without readers like you, it would not be possible.